MW00636116

Death Ride

Death Ride:

A Little Boy's Night of Terror

To Gayle & Tom

All our best to you

Tim and Becky Hattenburg

Tim Hattenburg

Becky Hattenburg

Tornado Creek Publications
Spokane, Washington 2014

© 2014 Tim and Becky Hattenburg
All rights reserved, including the rights to translate or reproduce
this work or parts thereof in any form or by media, without
prior written permission from the authors

Printed by Sheridan Books, Inc.
Chelsea, Michigan

ISBN: 978-0-9821529-4-2

Library of Congress Control Number: 2014954572

Front cover photos:
Mike and Frieda Kuntz's wedding photo taken
November 26, 1929, in Richardton, North Dakota.
Inset:
Larry Kuntz, age five, in Wheat Basin, Montana,
with his dog Shep
(Photos courtesy Larry Kuntz)

TORNADO CREEK
PUBLICATIONS
Tony and Suzanne Bamonte
P.O. Box 8625
Spokane, Washington 99203
(509) 838-7114, Fax (509) 455-6798
www.tornadocreekpublications.com

Table of Contents

About the Authors

Tim and Becky Hattenburg have lived in Spokane Valley, Washington, most of their 41 years of marriage. They have two sons, Bobby and Justin, and a daughter Erica. Also, added to the family are son-in-law J. B. Hendon, daughter-in-law Kim Britton and three grandchildren.

Tim was born in Spokane and raised in the Spokane Valley. He graduated from Central Valley High School. Tim then graduated from Spokane Falls Community College and Washington State University with majors in history and education. He taught and coached at North Pines Junior High in the Spokane Valley until his retirement. Since then, Tim has done research for Tony and Suzanne Bamonte and Tornado Creek Publications. He is currently chair of the Spokane County Library District board of trustees and is involved in numerous community activities.

Becky was raised on a wheat farm between Oakesdale and Garfield, Washington and graduated from Oakesdale High School. She then attended Spokane Falls Community College where she and Tim met. Becky then transferred to beauty school and received her Washington State cosmetology license. She worked in salons in Pullman and Spokane before returning to school to earn her instructors license. Becky taught at the Spokane Skills Center for eight years and then opened a beauty school. She recently sold her share of the school and is semi-retired. Becky enjoys traveling with Tim and working on their new adventure of writing.

This book started out as a challenge, but after meeting Larry and Janet Kuntz, it became a labor of love.

Preface

This is the terrifying, heartbreaking, true story of Larry Kuntz and his parents, Mike and Frieda Kuntz. It tells of the survival of a five-year-old boy who was beaten and left for dead after having witnessed the murder of his parents in his father's car.

The young, happy family was living in the small town of Wheat Basin, Montana during the autumn of 1937. This rural community was outraged by the murders of the Kuntzes. Little did they suspect it was one of their own that took the family on a death ride that fateful Friday after Thanksgiving.

The following account covers the events that led up to the brutal murders, as well as the daunting task faced by the local sheriff's office, without the benefit of today's technology, in solving this vicious crime. It also exposes the eventual distorted confession and recounts the hanging of an escaped felon, whose wife and children had no prior knowledge of his sordid past.

This story also tells of the life of Larry Kuntz after his recovery from his near-death beating. This little boy was stripped of any semblance of a normal childhood and was left with having to endure nightmares for many years.

There have been many articles written regarding these events, and lacking an eyewitness, sometimes what authorities thought happened was based on conjecture by those involved in solving this case. It was not until about 2010 that an eyewitness was able to finally talk about what had really happened and fill in some of the missing facts or pieces of the puzzle regarding the night of the murders. That eyewitness is none other than Larry Kuntz himself.

Introduction

Wheat Basin used to be a town. But the weather, the bugs, and the evil that man can do all conspired to end its existence. The death of the town was gradual, but once a certain point was reached in size and population, it was inevitable. All that remains are a very few foundations and fading memories.

This is a harsh land, but it holds a majesty that is hard to comprehend without standing on it. Flat, but far from featureless, the ground is rugged and broken, sculpted by water, wind, and time. It is frozen in sudden gullies, ripples, and low ridges.

This is also speed goat territory, a local term used to describe the antelope that populate the area. It turns out that they are more closely related to goats than to deer or elk.

I stood by the foundation of the old Occident Grain Elevator with its rusted scales. This is all that remains from the fire that had burned it to the ground. I thought of what had brought my wife and me to this ghost of a town on the flat land of Eastern Montana. I was here for a new friend that we almost didn't meet. I was here to honor his memories, and to bring my journey to Wheat Basin full circle.

"You have to meet Larry," was the pronouncement from a longtime mentor of mine. She knew my love of history and my passion for looking into old records to solve some of the many mysteries time leaves us. We would find much to talk about, she told me. Larry has a story that needs to be told and you should be the one to tell it.

So, we met Larry and his family, and over the months, came to truly appreciate and love the gentle, kind man of 80-plus years. Beneath the humor and genuine warmth of this retired pharmacist was a tragedy from his childhood that he had kept buried deep in his soul until about eight years ago. Our first meeting with Larry and his wife, Janet, was as sad as it was wonderful. They were so open with us, sharing their memories as well as their photos. Larry didn't think his story was special enough to have a book written about it, but was willing to let us try, as long as the truth was told.

Acknowledgements

First we would like to thank our good friends and publishers, Tony and Suzanne Bamonte, who helped and encouraged us throughout the entire process of writing this book. Their expertise and knowledge in not only publishing, but also as authors, helped us tremendously.

Ian Graham edited and contributed his ideas and research to help make this book even more interesting. We also would like to thank Barbara Lomax, Erica Hendon, and Kristi Kuntz for their help with content and editing.

A big thank you goes to Penny Redli for all her help and allowing us access to the archives in the Museum of the Beartooths.

Thank you to Sally Jackson for telling us about Larry's story and encouraging us to write it.

We appreciate the photograph contributors, who are acknowledged in the photo captions.

Dedication

This book is dedicated to Larry and Janet Kuntz and their wonderful family, without whom this project would have been impossible. We would like to thank them for all the help they have given us. It is an honor to have met them and to now count them as our friends.

Chapter One

Wheat Basin

As five-year-old Larry slowly came to, he tried to open his swollen, blackened eyes through the blood that had dried on his face. His head ached terribly, his hands hurt as though they had been crushed, and he felt the dull throb of a cramp in his leg. He had never been in so much pain.

Larry could feel carpeting under his hands. The smell of oil filled his nostrils and the hard metal of a seat support against his leg gradually helped him realize he was in the family car. His recollection of how he came to be on the floor in the back of his papa's car seemed hazy. All he could feel at this moment was extreme pain and intense cold. As he tried to remember, and in a semiconscious state, he took himself back to his first memories of Wheat Basin.

Drifting in and out of consciousness, his mind wandered. He remembered sitting in the car with his mama, watching papa drive them to their new home in Wheat Basin, Montana. The memory was still bright, like the button his mama had sewn onto his coat. He had been happy and comfortable in the memory, or at least as comfortable as one could be while breathing dust and bouncing around in the car, thrown about at the mercy of the rutted road.

The memory was from about eight months ago, in the early spring of 1937. The flat land they were driving through seemed to go on forever, but the car kept jolting along, following the dirt track worn into the hard ground. The family was moving to a new town.

Larry had brought his dog Shep with him because, sometimes having lived where there were not very many kids to play with, Shep had be-

Mike, Larry, and Frieda outside of their home in Beulah, North Dakota, 1934. Notice Larry's toy wagon to the left of Mike. *(Courtesy Larry Kuntz.)*

come his best friend. They were always together, exploring and playing outside. The move to this new town was a chance for them to explore even more places. Larry was so excited he could hardly sit still. This was going to be a great adventure, he was just sure of it.

The year 1937 had brought some changes to the town of Wheat Basin, located in the eastern part of the state, midway between the communities of Molt and Rapelje. The nearest towns of any size were those of Columbus (pop. 800) 26 miles to the south and the much larger city of Billings (pop. 20,000), which was about 40 miles to the east. The town site was made up of approximately 60 residents, consisting mostly of the store owners and their families. Wheat Basin was on the decline due to drought conditions and a struggling economy, forcing many residents to move away to larger populated areas with the hopes of finding better employment opportunities.

A large corporation called the Occident Grain Company had purchased one of the two grain elevators located just on the south end of town and had hired a man from North Dakota to be the new manager. The month of April arrived and so did Mike Kuntz, along with his wife, Frieda, and Larry, their five-year-old son. When Mike received his job offer to manage the Occident Elevator, the Kuntz family had packed up their belongings, loaded them into the car, and made the long, (approximately 450 miles) arduous drive from their former residence in Beulah, North Dakota, to Wheat Basin. Mike had previous experience in the grain elevator business, having worked at elevators in Antelope from 1929 to 1934, and Beulah, from 1935 to 1936.

Mike and Frieda were hesitant to make the move, but the pay was good. During these difficult years of the Great Depression, you took what work you could find. They had both come from large, close-knit families and leaving them all behind was hard to do.

Frieda and Mike just weeks after their wedding in Richardton, North Dakota, 1929. *(Courtesy Larry Kuntz.)*

Mike Kuntz was born in Richardton, North Dakota, on January 26, 1903, and had been educated at St. Mary's School and Assumption Abbey Col-

A montage of photos of Larry Kuntz and his parents, Mike and Frieda, in the mid-1930s, during happier times. *(Courtesy Larry Kuntz.)*

lege in Richardton. For a time he was employed as a grocery clerk in his hometown before working at grain elevators.

Frieda Hammerschmidt Kuntz was born in Richardton in 1909 and educated in Richardton schools. Later, the Peoples Telephone Company of Taylor and Richardton employed her as chief operator, a position three of her sisters – Genevieve, Louise, and Eleanor – went on to hold. On November 26, 1929, she was married to Mike Kuntz in Richardton.

Arriving in Wheat Basin late in the evening, after about a twelve-hour drive, the family located the very modest house they would call home. It was about one block from the grain elevator where Mike was the new manager.

Mike Kuntz on a jumping board while he was in school at the Abbey in Richardton, circa 1920. Mike was exhibiting his athletic skills. *(Courtesy Larry Kuntz.)*

Mike and Frieda were a bit disappointed to find that the small house had no electricity or telephone and, worse yet, there was no well for fresh water. Deciding they could find out later where the water supply was, Mike built a fire in the stove. He and Frieda laughed at Larry as he rejoiced at not having to take a bath that night.

It was very common for most people living in rural areas throughout the entire country not to have indoor plumbing or electricity during this time period. Although 90 percent of urban dwellers had electricity by the 1930s, only about 10 percent of rural residents did. The federal government created the Rural Electrification Act (REA) of 1935 in order to bring electricity to hundreds of thousands of people living outside of urban areas. It was not until the end of World War II in 1945 that a majority of residents living in rural areas had been connected to the electric grid through the efforts of the REA.

General stores found in the small towns often doubled as the location of the local post office. These stores were usually a place for the towns-people to gather for local gossip and news from the "outside world". The Hindenburg disaster in May and the disappearance of Amelia Earhart in early July gave people lots to talk about.

Early the next morning, the Kuntz family went about exploring the small town. They discovered that any remaining businesses were lo-cated on the one and only main street. A church, the now-empty bank building, and post office were located at a midway point between Mike Visser's general store and their home. Just past Visser's store was the Simpkins Lumber Company, near the end of the main street. Beyond the lumberyard and its dwindling piles of stock, the road then curved on its rutted path to Columbus.

The U.S. Postal Service, due to the declining population of the small community, had closed the post office the previous year, in 1936. Con-sequently, the mail was brought to the general store by a mail carrier, Ira Reams, from Billings. There was a community hall, located a block off the main street, where an occasional dance was held for the enter-tainment of the residents. These events were becoming less frequent as the population of the area continued its downward spiral. The small schoolhouse and Catholic church were the only other public buildings scattered among the family homes that made up the rest of the town.

This area had not escaped the effects of the Great Depression, which began on Black Tuesday, October 29, 1929. The bottom had fallen out of the stock market and banks were failing throughout the nation. As a result, securing loans for crops had become very difficult. Since then, times had been very hard. Many millions of people were out of work, with few areas in the country left untouched.

Many times transients from other states, who were making their way west for a chance at employment, would show up looking for work with farmers, who could not afford to hire them. Families in rural ar-eas who had lived on and farmed the land were especially hard hit as they had nowhere to go and few job opportunities. The unemployment rate across the country in the mid 1930s was as high as 25 percent.

Literacy beyond the basics was rare. Very few farm families had the skills or training to find jobs in urban industrial areas. So, the families hung on and prayed for the weather to cooperate and the crops to come in. One by one, farms were foreclosed by the banks or creditors and their land, as well as their farm equipment, was auctioned off or repossessed, forcing families to move away. In 1933, the average person living in the area earned only $145 a year. That compared with a national average of $375, over twice as much. Making matters worse, there were severe droughts that had lasted for several years, dramatically impacting the yield of the wheat crops.

As such, Mike Kuntz felt fortunate to be employed and have a steady paycheck to take care of his small family. The future of his employment meant being willing to move Frieda and Larry, on more than a few occasions, to some very small towns in remote areas.

The previous manager had also informed Mike that many of the farmers had already borrowed money against unharvested crops. Therefore, he would need to go over all the records at his new office to check on who was to receive money and who had liens against the grain they were to deliver to his elevator. Managing a grain elevator in wheat country was serious business. His job combined the responsibility of banker, buyer, and business manager.

The Occident Elevator was in competition with the Farmers Elevator Company, which was located right alongside it by the railroad tracks. Given this situation, Mike was under even more pressure to make a profit for the Occident Company, as well as to provide a fair price to the farmers. This was made even more difficult since crop prices were so low due to the distressed economy.

With this challenging task ahead of him, Mike went about familiarizing himself with the records and receipts, as well as his potential customers. He made friends effortlessly and was well-liked and respected by those who came to know him. Individual farmers who dealt with Mike were not surprised that he was a very fair and honest man and would do everything he could to help them out. As manager of the elevator, it was also understood that he was unable to extend further loans or credit when they had liens against their grain in storage or on crops that had not yet been harvested.

In researching the records and receipts from past years, Mike discovered that up until 1921 the farmers around Wheat Basin averaged about 20 bushels of wheat per acre. Primarily because of severe weather, that number had dropped dramatically to 8-12 bushels per acre. The last

Larry's grandmother Mary Kuntz; Genevieve, Frieda's sister; Frieda and Larry at a family gathering just before they moved to Wheat Basin in the spring of 1937. *(Courtesy Larry Kuntz.)*

three years had been especially hard on the community as a whole, with no relief in sight. The spring wheat crop had dried out and all that was left to harvest was the winter wheat, which also looked to be a very meager crop. Facing a dismal and uncertain future, Mike told Frieda that he hated the prospect of living here for any length of time and would seek another place of employment if necessary. But work was work, and Mike buckled down to the long hours at the elevator.

With Mike hard at work, Frieda and Larry were left to unpack and put their place in order. Frieda was a fastidious homemaker, and it took her very little time to clean and have everything perfectly arranged. Even though their small house was sparsely furnished, it looked especially cozy after Frieda finished decorating.

One of the most repetitious and tedious tasks that Mike had was to travel nearly two miles every day in order to bring fresh water to their home in a five-gallon metal milk can. This was not unusual in this area. The alkalinity of the ground water made it unsafe for human consumption, so the drinking water from sweet wells was precious. Mike had to duplicate this effort in order to obtain fresh milk and cream.

The work week was six full days, so Sunday was family day. On Sundays, after attending services at the Catholic church, Mike would sit Larry on his lap, and they would read the comic section of the newspaper together. Popeye, Little Orphan Annie, and Buck Rodgers were Larry's favorites. His papa was just letting him get into Dick Tracy, too. Mike liked Krazy Kat, but Larry didn't understand much of the humor in it. He did think the drawings were fun though.

Frieda would busily prepare a nice family dinner for all to enjoy. On special occasions, she would spring for the expense of chicken. At 20 cents a pound, it was a luxury they enjoyed greatly, but rarely. More commonly, they would have a hamburger loaf that cost a more affordable 12 cents a pound. She was a master at making one-pot casseroles that were very tasty, but also frugal. Frieda was an adventurous cook. She was thinking about introducing the family to the brand new Hormel product just introduced that year. It was called Spam, and was all the rage in the cities.

Being a family day, they would many times go for a drive when the weather permitted. Exploring their new home area, always trying to go somewhere different, was exciting for Larry. Mike especially enjoyed going to the areas of Montana that had lots of green grass and trees.

Larry and his mother Frieda outside their home in Wheat Basin. They had just returned from church on a spring Sunday afternoon in 1937. *(Courtesy Larry Kuntz)*

For instance, their first weekend found the family driving south to the mountains. Mike and Frieda both agreed "how dandy" things looked out there. They drove through valleys and along rivers with fresh clean water and plenty of green grass and vegetation. Mike told Frieda that he would someday like to live there if he could own one of the farms in that area. He went on to share with her that if the Occident Company would not place him somewhere in the valley, he would not even want to stay in Wheat Basin through the coming winter. "If that is not a possibility, I would rather take you and Larry back to North Dakota and resume our lives there. I am already growing tired of the sagebrush, gumbo soil, rattlesnakes, and alkali water," Mike told the family.

Frieda and Larry met a few of their neighbors. Frank and May Robideau lived very near to them. Frank was a tenant farmer and also the local distributor for Zanol products. This was a door-to-door line of food, cosmetics, and household products from Cincinnati. Frank was often away and worked long hours for little return.

Larry quickly made friends with one of the Robideaus' three children, Richard. As the two boys were about the same age, they soon became frequent playmates. They were both excited to have someone with whom they could share their adventures in this small town.

Richard's mom, May, had recently found out she was expecting her fourth child in December. May was taking special care during this pregnancy because she and Frank had lost a three-year-old child to pneumonia in the previous winter. Frieda and May became so comfortable in their friendship that May asked Frieda to be the midwife during the delivery of her baby. It was not unusual for babies to be delivered by midwives in small rural areas throughout the entire country. With the nearest doctor at least 30 miles, with an hour or more drive, given the terrible road conditions in the winter, this gave some comfort to May. She would have someone with her at the time of her delivery. Frieda did not have any formal medical training. However, growing up with several younger siblings, she was comfortable with the birthing process and agreed to help May.

Larry, his dog Shep, and Richard had great fun that spring and summer exploring the desolate little town. Their moms constantly reminded them to be on the watch for rattlesnakes in the sagebrush. The boys especially enjoyed Mr. Visser's general store, where they would go to buy candy or other treats.

Frieda Kuntz, standing next to their car in the slushy snow on the road to Wheat Basin in November 1937. Photo taken by Mike Kuntz. *(Courtesy Larry Kuntz)*

The Kuntz home in Wheat Basin, Montana. *(Courtesy Victor Murphy)*

On one occasion, not having the necessary funds, they hatched a scheme to raise money in order to purchase some candy. In their explorations of the area, Larry and Richard had come across an empty Prince Albert to-bacco tin. Richard told Larry that his father, Frank Robideau, regularly smoked cigarettes rolled with tobacco from a tin similar to this. They reasoned that if they could fill it with something that resembled the dried tobacco, they could sell it to raise their "candy money." The two young entrepreneurs went about searching for their ingredients and came upon an old fence post that had rotted to the point of being sawdust, resembling a tobacco-like texture. Eureka! They carefully filled their tin with the mixture, assured that it would pass as tobacco, and set out to find a potential buyer.

One of the many ads that the Prince Albert tobacco company placed in various newspapers and magazines in the 1930s. They advertised as "the easy-to-roll joy smoke." *(The Spokesman-Review, circa 1937)*

As luck would have it, Richard's dad was the first person they came across. Coyly approaching him, the two boys smiled and presented the old rusty can crammed with sawdust. Frank opened the can and laughingly declined the purchase. He obviously had failed to fall for the "sawdust as tobacco" scam. Even though the boys decided they would need to refine their skills in obtaining funds for their candy, they had fun trying.

With the railroad trains arriving only once a week to swap out the cars filled with grain, it could be pretty quiet and life in this small hamlet uneventful. In a letter to his brother Val, Mike pointed out that Frieda was unable to have her much-anticipated vegetable garden and likened the texture of the soil to that of gumbo, thick and gooey when wet and unable to hold moisture below the surface when dry. Gumbo was the term commonly used in eastern Montana by the locals in describing the dirt roads when they were wet from a rainstorm.

Frieda was disappointed with this finding, as she had always enjoyed serving fresh vegetables to her family and in the fall months being able to store the extras for the upcoming winter. Not only were the canned vegetables tasty, but helped ease the day-to-day expenses. Canned peas or corn sold at 2 for 29 cents. Peaches were even more at 39 cents for 2 cans, which was almost more than their budget could handle.

She had also enjoyed raising chickens; however, they did not have any sheds or barns to shelter them, so they would have to purchase fresh eggs elsewhere. Even with these drawbacks, as they quickly settled into the routine of their new home, the Kuntz family found themselves welcomed and people to be very friendly.

Larry loved to dress up as a cowboy and play with his dog Shep. He especially liked to wear his new cowboy boots when he went to Visser's store with his mother. Photo taken at their Wheat Basin home during the late summer of 1937. *(Courtesy Larry Kuntz)*

Larry and his papa, Mike, in Mike's grain elevator office in Beulah, North Dakota, 1936. This office was nearly identical to the one in Wheat Basin. *(Courtesy Larry Kuntz)*

One day a week Frieda did her shopping at the general store, which also served as the post office where she could pick up their mail. Larry loved shopping day. He would walk with his mama the quarter mile distance in his new cowboy boots, and Mike Visser, the store owner, would always give him a special treat (chocolate was his favorite) while Frieda got the supplies she needed for the week.

When Larry wasn't helping his mom or playing with his new friend Richard Robideau, he would go to the grain elevator with his papa. It was a wonderful place to make up all kinds of games. Larry explored every inch of the elevator that his papa allowed him to play in. The elevator was like a giant castle that had landed here just for him. For a little boy who was only about three and a half feet tall, the 80 foot silo on the elevator was daunting in its enormity.

Larry took great interest in watching his papa load the grain cars. When Mike would go into the grain storage areas to load up the bags of wheat onto a handcart and disappear into darkness, Larry felt like he was holding his breath until his papa would reappear with a smile on his face for his son. Larry grew to love the musty odor from the dust of the grain as Mike unhooked the latch on a large sliding door leading to the loading platform, where he took the bags of grain to be loaded onto a railroad car. Little did that five-year-old boy know the time he spent exploring the elevator would soon save his life.

Some Saturdays, toward the end of the day, Mike would be in a playful mood. He was a huge fan of Charlie Chaplin. He adored "the little tramp"

and had a particular fondness for one of Chaplain's short films "The Waiter." So, Mike would put on a coat, drape a white towel over his arm, and climb to the top of the grain elevator. There was a window at the top with a beam extending out just above it. The beam had a pulley on it so loads could be hoisted up to the top. Mike would lean out the window, grab the beam, and hang by one hand 60 feet over the hard ground, as he would mime the duck-footed walk of Chaplin. Larry thought that was great fun. Frieda would never yell when she caught Mike showing off like that, but she did have a scary feeling in the pit of her stomach when she saw him hanging out of the elevator window with the 60 foot drop below him.

Mike loved Charlie Chaplin and would occasionally dress up like him and clown around. Photo taken at Antelope, North Dakota, circa 1935. *(Courtesy Larry Kuntz)*

As summer arrived and the fields of wheat changed from green to golden, a hailstorm went through the area, causing more damage to the already meager crops. July and August were still extremely dry months, with less than .5 of an inch of rain in July and .15 of an inch for August; September was only slightly better with .75 of an inch. On the plains of eastern Montana, about 12-15 inches of rain is average. During the drought years of the depression era, rainfall dropped as much as 25 percent.

A drought of a year or so was a survivable event. But severe droughts that lasted for several years dramatically impacted the yield of the precious wheat crops. To the dry-land farmers in the Wheat Basin area who were already living a marginal existence, the prolonged drought spelled disaster.

As if this was not enough for the farmers to deal with, there had been an infestation of grasshoppers and Mormon crickets throughout most of Still-water County, which caused severe crop losses. The Mormon cricket is a large flightless grasshopper that grows to almost three inches long. They swarm in densities of a hundred per square yard and travel almost one and a half miles a day. With grasshoppers attacking in the millions, there is little that can be done to deter these menaces, even today. With these grim events, the grain had to be cut and harvest was in full swing with the farmers bringing in their sparse crops of wheat to Mike's elevator.

When the harvest season finished, Mike was still very busy at the elevator, buying, selling, and storing wheat, then shipping it out by rail, while keeping up with the necessary book work. Larry didn't mind papa's long hours, because he could spend even more time with him at the elevator playing in his make-believe castle.

The arrival of fall found the farmers around the area busy plowing their fields and getting the ground ready to plant the winter wheat crop for

Mike dressed as Charlie Chaplin, doing Chaplin's famous walk from "The Waiter." He was hanging about 60 feet above the ground from a window in the Occident Grain Elevator while Frieda took his photo. *(Courtesy Larry Kuntz)*

Mike Kuntz in a tree in Richardton, circa 1918. *(Courtesy Larry Kuntz)*

the next year. Winter wheat is a tougher variety and is planted in the fall, allowing it to catch the moisture from the autumn rains. This type of wheat has to go through a cold spell in order to produce the seed on the head of the plant. When the snow falls, and the ground is frozen, the plant goes dormant. The springtime sun and warmth bring the wheat back into its growth cycle, allowing for its harvest in the summer.

Once the crops were planted in the late fall, the farmers had time off from the fields. This was no vacation on a working farm. It meant it was time to perform the necessary maintenance needed on their equipment. This was long, cold work that would last them through the winter months.

In the economic cycle of a farm town, late fall was particularly important. It was when farmers received payment for their crops. In many cases, that money had already been spent.

Store merchants liked the post harvest season, too, as farmers could at last pay off the credit accounts that most of them had to establish. They looked forward to having some cash customers again, even if only until the money ran out.

The cycle was normal for the time period in numerous rural communities throughout the entire country and farmers, for many years to come, continued to face this dilemma. Borrowing money against the next year's crops is still a common practice in many farming communities today. Many of these people are tenant farmers who lease land from other individuals or corporations. The rent is then paid to the owners either in cash or from a share of the crop when it is harvested and sold. Almost a quarter of the farmers around Wheat Basin were tenants.

One of the local tenant farmers that season, who was having an especially hard time financially, was the Kuntz's neighbor, Frank Robideau. His farm machinery had been repossessed, consequently, he had to hire others to harvest his crop at a great personal expense.

Knowing everything in his name was being taken due to lack of payment, in August of 1937, Frank went to Columbus. At the county courthouse, he changed the name on the house he owned in Wheat Basin to his wife's name. The Robideaus were hoping this would keep creditors from taking their home away. Although other farmers in the area were also having a hard time financially, they did not resort to the drastic measures that Robideau would take that late autumn.

Frieda (left) and one of her six sisters, Rose, in Richardton, North Dakota, circa 1934. *(Courtesy Larry Kuntz)*

Chapter Two

A Night of Terror

November 26, 1937, was crisp and cold. The winter was going to be a long one; all the old folks said so. Mike Kuntz blew on his hands to warm them and looked at the ledger he was working on. The neat rows of figures and his aching hand let him know it was late. He was hungry, and the thought of getting home brought a smile to his tired face. Despite being the day after Thanksgiving, he had worked a full day at the elevator, tending to the paperwork that seemed to never end. The small stove in the office space didn't do enough to keep him warm, let alone make a dent in the chill of the larger space of the elevator. He straightened up, easing a strain in his back from the hard chair. Mike wondered what he was going to do to keep warm in the deep winter to come.

Mike was just starting to wrap up his work, filing the account ledgers and shipping manifest, when Frank Robideau walked into the elevator office. Frank was a small man, with a wiry five-foot five-inch frame that was deceptively strong. He had a thin face, with a wild shock of dark hair and a full beard. He tended to dart about, nervously looking around, but this afternoon his manners were even more twitchy than normal. Mike immediately knew something was very wrong. Frank was sweating, despite the chill, and Mike noticed that Frank was glancing about as if he feared the shadows would jump out at him.

In a quick voice cracking with tension, Frank demanded Mike do something about his financial problems. At first, Mike had trouble understanding what Frank wanted. Eventually, he pieced together from Frank's confusing rant that he was to write a check for grain Frank claimed he had stored at the elevator. Mike quickly double-checked all the records, but it was clear that Frank was wrong. He had already borrowed against the grain. Frank was broke.

When Mike explained the Occident Company didn't owe Frank any money because of the liens on his grain, Frank became extremely angry and pulled out a .38 caliber pistol and pointed it at him. Mike immediately froze, and he began to think this situation was deadly serious. Although Frank was nervous, the gun and the hand that held it were steady and Frank's face showed a grim determination. Mike couldn't believe it. Was Frank trying to hold him up for cash? Mike didn't have any cash on hand, in person or at the facility. Frank would know that.

With a crafty look on his face, Frank told him to write a series of checks and to make them out in various farmers' names. Frank explained that he would then endorse and cash them. Mike didn't argue with the clearly disturbed man. He was not about to get shot over some worthless paper. There wasn't enough cash in the whole town to cover these checks, so Mike agreed with Frank's demands.

As Mike started writing, Frank warned him not to go to the authorities in Columbus, or he would hunt him and his family down and shoot them all. Mike didn't know Frank that well, but he could tell by the menacing look in his dark eyes that he meant what he said. He wrote faster. He just wanted to get home and make sure Larry and Frieda were safe.

Mike knew there was no one in the town that could do anything about Frank. If he hollered for help, making a scene now would only cause Frank to get more violent. Frank was clearly out of control, and the best thing to do was to get away from him and hope he cooled down some. Any possible help was 26 miles away, which would have taken at least an hour. Mike did what he could to get through the coming night.

Back at home, Larry was looking forward to his papa coming home so the family could have supper. He hovered in the small living room, peering into the kitchen. He always loved the smells of the freshly cooked foods that permeated the air in their small kitchen and throughout the house. This was especially true as tonight there were treats left over from Thanksgiving to be had. Frieda smiled at Larry's antics. She too was looking forward to Mike coming home.

Frieda glanced out the window, but saw only the blankness of night beyond the frame and her nice curtains. It got dark early here on the prairie, and there were only a few dim glows from distant windows dotting the gathering dark. Frieda felt very alone, and she was glad Mike would be home soon.

When Mike came in, he was unusually tense. Larry noticed this and could tell his papa had something to say to his mama. He didn't press for news though. He knew he'd have to wait. There was a long standing rule in the family. Dinner was not to be interrupted. Food was too precious, and to Mike and Frieda, so was the family time together that meals provided. Worries, joys, and important news would all be put aside until after dinner. As Mike cleaned up at the washtub, he drew the shades. He was going to share with his wife the harrowing experience he had just been through, just as soon as dinner was over and Larry could be safely kept busy in the living room.

Larry came to the table eagerly. With his papa home and his mama setting the table with dishes and platters of food, he felt safe and secure.

No sooner had Mike said their customary blessing than there was a loud knock on the front door. Mike looked concerned but reluctantly opened the door. Frank shouldered his way into the Kuntz residence, and as he walked into the kitchen area, they immediately saw he had a gun in his hand. Larry recognized this man as Frank Robideau, the father of his favorite playmate, Richard.

Frieda gave a muffled cry of fear. She was terrified of guns. She knew from her friend May that Frank had a temper, but this was not an anger she understood. The sight of Robideau, waving the pistol in the air and talking loudly, filled her with dread. She recognized the raw edge of madness in Frank. He soon ordered Mike, herself, and Larry into the living room.

Mr. Robideau engaged Mike in a wild discourse about the evils of the Occident Grain Company and about some money he claimed the grain company alledgedly owed him. Mike was very worried now. Clearly Frank was not cooling off. Instead, he was getting more and more agitated. The safety of Larry and Frieda was now Mike's top priority.

Frank Robideau, around the time he entered the Kuntz home on the fateful night of November 1937. *(Courtesy Victor Murphy, Museum of the Beartooths)*

Speaking in a calm, even voice, Mike was able to eventually convince Frank that he should sit down and discuss his concerns in a civil manner or leave the premises. As Frank sat, Larry was very frightened to see him holding the gun in his hands between his knees while continuing his rambling, disjointed argument with his father. He didn't understand all of what they were saying, but he did react to the ugly expression and the wild tone of Frank's voice. Larry just wanted his friend's dad to leave. He would talk to Richard about this tomorrow.

Mike tried everything he could, desperately trying to save his family. Nothing seemed to work. Suddenly, Frank stood up with the gun pointed at Mike and demanded that the family go outside to their car as they were all "going for a drive."

Wary of Frank's motives, the family reluctantly stood and walked toward the door. Frank jabbed the gun at Frieda, but she gave him a glare that Larry knew was reserved for the very worst of times. He had last seen it when he spilled milk while fooling around and carelessly swinging a stick he had picked up. Frieda stubbornly stopped and turned to hand Mike and Larry their coats, then grabbed her own coat and pocketbook. Frank briefly looked a little sorry for his actions.

On the short walk to the car, Larry thought it was strangely quiet. He didn't hear another human sound in the frigid night, and he looked longingly for a light so someone else might see what was happening. There was none. The night was still and dark, with only the wind as a witness.

Frank directed Mike to get in the driver's seat of the well-worn Chevy, and when Frieda tried to sit in back with Larry, he motioned for her to move her hand back to the handle of the front door. "You sit with Mike. Larry will sit with me," he ordered.

He then placed Larry in the back seat with him, making him sit directly behind Frieda. Frieda and Mike didn't want Frank back there with their little boy, but they had no choice. As Mike started the car and slowly pulled out onto the rutted road, Larry heard the crunch made by the tires on the frozen clumps of mud that made up the road. As they jolted along, the bug-eyed headlights of the Chevy cast a narrow cone of light into the dark night.

Frank casually put the gun in the inside pocket of his jacket. Following Frank's terse directions, they headed out of town towards Columbus, and Mike's heart sank. He knew this was not going to end well. He realized that he might not even have enough gas in the tank to make it to Columbus.

Larry normally loved going for a ride in the car. This usually meant they were going to visit friends, relatives or even go on a family adventure. This time, however, things felt very different. The father of his best friend was forcing them to go for a drive. The man was scary. He not only had a gun, but also a mean look on his face. Larry didn't want to be sitting right next to him. He wanted to be in the front seat with his mama and papa, as he normally would have done. This frightened the little boy and the tension in the adults made the car ride even more miserable. His mama was continually looking over her shoulder, and Mike took every opportunity he could to glance in the rear view mirror, hoping to detect any movement from the darkened interior of the vehicle.

To Larry, it seemed like it was ages, but only ten or twelve miles out of Wheat Basin, Frank suddenly directed Mike to pull over. "I want a smoke," he said.

As Mike slowed the car to a stop and turned off the engine, Frank reached inside his jacket pocket. Instead of pulling out a cigarette, he pulled out his .38 caliber special and in one smooth motion, placed the cold steel of the gun barrel at the base of Mike's skull and pulled the trigger.

The blinding flash and deafening bang of the gun going off in the closed car made Larry freeze in terror. Frieda screamed. She knew Mike was dead. Blood had splattered all over the side window and he lay slumped against the steering wheel, blood pouring from his head. Frieda knew she and Larry would be next if she was unable to disarm Robideau.

Desperately, Frieda lunged back over the seat at Robideau in a frantic effort to save her little boy. She put everything she had into an attempt to grab Frank's hand and get the gun.

"Larry, RUN!"

The cry from his mama jolted Larry into action. He threw open the car door and took a few steps into the blackness surrounding the car. In his fear and desperation he was turned around and confused about his direction.

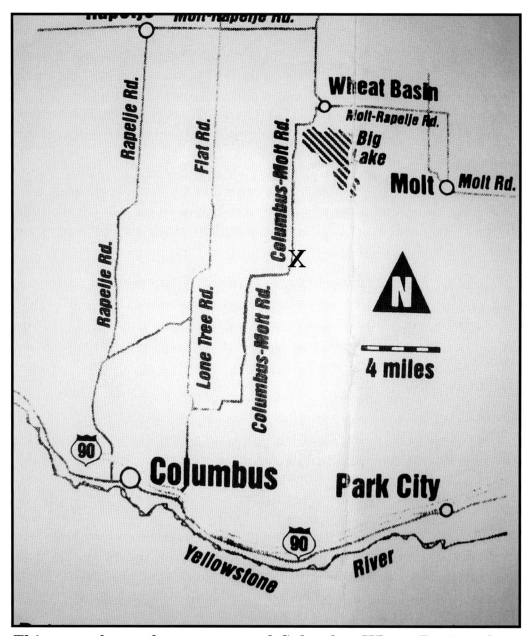

This map shows the area around Columbus/Wheat Basin, where Robideau had Mike Kuntz pull his car over was just before the second sharp corner on the Columbus–Molt Road (X marks the spot on the map). *(Map Courtesy the Columbus News)*

Frieda continued to struggle and fight with Frank in any way possible. Frank hit Frieda in the face and fired his pistol in an attempt to shoot her. Frieda saw the strobe of the muzzle flash and felt more then heard the sharp bang of the shot. The round went through the car roof. Frieda fought on desperately. She bit into the hand that was clutching the gun.

Larry ran toward the front of the car, where the headlights illuminated the darkness. Inside the car, another shot was fired. Once more, a bullet narrowly missed Frieda and struck the post over the windshield. Another shot was fired, this time the bullet going into the side pocket of the door. He fired his last bullet, this time piercing Frieda's heart – exiting her body through her left shoulder blade. This final round left a hole in the windshield. Instantly, her valiant effort to save herself and her young son was over.

Frank jumped out of the back seat in pursuit. Larry could hear the heavy steps directly behind. As he attempted to run, a sharp jerk on his collar stopped him in his tracks. Now, Larry on shaking little legs was alone, terrified – and caught.

Larry struggled desperately, but Frank was too strong. His head exploded in pain as Robideau brought the butt of the now-empty revolver handle down on his head. The blows came fast and furiously. In a desperate attempt to protect himself, Larry covered his head with his hands hoping to ward off the blows. It didn't work. Blow after blow dazed him, each strike bringing new pain and new agony. Then came another blow, this one to the side of his head, and Larry's world went dark.

Frank continued to beat the unconscious boy while dragging him back to the car. Flinging the now limp little body into the back seat, he watched as blood began to pool around Larry's head. Positive that Larry was dead, he quickly slammed the door, leaving himself standing alone in the night.

Surveying the scene, Frank realized that he needed to conjure up a plan to conceal this crime and his role in it. Walking around to the front passenger door, Frank opened it. Frieda's body was lying halfway over the seat she had been in. He pushed her until she fell onto the floor of the backseat. Moving around to the driver's side, he nudged the body of Mike over just enough for his small frame to fit behind the wheel of the car. The blood from Mike's head wound had soaked the seat. More had run out onto the running board and stained the dirt beneath the car. Frank had no choice but to sit there in the rapidly cooling pool of blood in order to drive the car.

As he grabbed the steering wheel, Frank could feel his hands stick to it from the blood of his victims. With his hands shaking from the adrenaline rush his actions had fostered, Frank turned the key and the car motor rumbled to life. He then turned the car around and slowly drove back toward the town of Wheat Basin and the Occident Grain Elevator. Frank knew there were no witnesses to the events that had taken place at the grain elevator earlier that day. He and Mike had been alone. He also knew there were no witnesses to the cold-blooded murders of the Kuntz family on this isolated road. Now he needed a place to hide the car with the bodies inside. It had to be a place where some time would pass before they were discovered. Time, he needed time to distance himself from the crime and to establish an alibi.

Frank thought of the empty grain elevator. There was plenty of room to park the car on the scales used for weighing trucks. It was inside and out of view. Being a close neighbor of Mike Kuntz, Frank knew that Mike would often park his car in the driveway of the elevator and walk the short distance to his home. During inclement weather he was known to park the car inside the elevator. If anyone did notice the car there, it would not seem unusual. Yes, that was it. He would lock the Chevy in the grain elevator, where the car and bodies would remain undetected. Perhaps it would take the whole weekend before they were found.

Who could he blame for the murders? Frank thought of events in town recently and couldn't think of anyone else who had argued with Mike. Mike was simply too well liked for it to be plausible someone else had killed him. Then Frank remembered the latest visitors to town. Two hitchhikers had come through, looking for work or food. They were just the latest in a steady trickle that came through, working their way west to warmer climates and the hope of employment. Frank would tell the police that the two hitchhikers seen by him and others in the area had probably been the ones who killed the Kuntz family. The hitchhikers would surely be long gone by the time the police discovered the bodies and went looking for them, and he would be in the clear.

As Frank drove, he hit several of the ruts in the road especially hard. He was not as skillful a driver as Mike had been. The jolts and the rough bouncing were enough to jostle Larry into partial consciousness for a few moments. Something was wrong with Larry's head. He couldn't see well and his thoughts felt fuzzy. He was scared, but he dared not make a sound. Very soon, the exhaustion, the pain, and loss of blood over powered him, and he drifted off again.

As he approached town, Frank's grip on the steering wheel tightened and his body tensed. He looked up and down the main street, hoping not to see anyone. It was very unlikely anyone would be out of his or her home on this dark, cold night. All the businesses closed at 5:00 p.m. and it was now after 8:00 p.m.. No one saw him driving Mike's car as he passed through town and pulled up to the elevator door. Frank hurriedly got out of the car and ran up the ramp to open the large door. The noise the doors made as they creaked open caused Frank to look around again. Seeing no one, he returned to the car and carefully drove it inside, parking it on the scales. Once safely inside he closed the large door. He made sure to leave the headlights of the car on so he could see Mike's roll top desk in the office. Frank searched through the office and found a piece of cardboard and a pencil. He scrawled a quick note that said, "We are closed today." Grabbing a hammer and nail off a shelf, he turned off the headlights, then slid the big door open just enough to squeeze through and exit the elevator. Outside once again, Frank closed the door and latched it from the outside. He attached the sign just above the handle, hoping this would keep anyone from looking for the Kuntz family for a day or so.

The handwritten note that Frank Robideau attached outside of the elevator door. It was meant to keep people from discovering the Kuntz car and their bodies, which he had hidden inside. *(Photo by Victor Murphy, Courtesy Museum of the Beartooths)*

Frank felt relief as he disappeared into the shadows left by the rising crescent moon, and hurriedly walked the short distance to his small house. Upon entering his home, he was pleased he had the foresight and planning to send May and the kids to a relative's house for the Thanksgiving holiday. Lighting the lantern on the table, he then realized how blood-soaked he was. There was blood on his hands and all over the front of him. His pants were soaked in blood from sitting on the front seat of the car on the drive back to the elevator. Frank knew he had to clean up and get rid of these clothes. Stoking up the fire in his wood-burning stove, he took off the bloodied clothes and threw them into the now-blazing fire.

Frank put on some clean clothes and felt his ordeal was finally coming to a close. His next order of business in his cover-up was to get rid of the gun. Going out into his back yard, he dug a hole just deep enough to conceal the gun and box of bullets that he had kept in the house. He then went back inside to check the stove to make sure his clothes had burned thoroughly. Using a fire poker, he sifted through the burnt remains and discovered that Mike's set of keys had been left in his pocket and now had been badly charred in the fire. He had to get rid of these!

Carefully removing the keys from the stove with the pointed edge of the fire poker, Frank took them outside. Digging once more into the frozen ground, he added them to the hole where he buried the gun. As Frank finished covering the hole, he probably breathed a sigh of relief. The ghostly feel of a hangman's noose around his neck was starting to fade. No one would ever know he had killed the Kuntz family. He had destroyed or hidden all the evidence.

He had planned this well, he thought. His first step had been making sure his wife and kids were out of town for the Thanksgiving holiday. This way, they would have no knowledge of the dastardly murders he had

The keys belonging to Mike Kuntz that Robideau unknowingly burned in his stove along with his blood-soaked clothes. He buried them in the backyard, along with the gun. They were given to Val Kuntz by Sheriff Murphy. *(Courtesy Richard Kuntz, Hattenburg photo)*

just committed. In addition, he had the bogus checks he had forced Mike to write at gunpoint to other farmers, which would validate his story. And finally, he had committed the murders on a stretch of empty road. The total of these actions would further disguise his part as the originator of the crime. At this time, he felt he had enough alibis to conceal his terrible crime. By now, Frank was exhausted and went to bed, knowing he had a few things left to do in the morning to complete his plan.

Awakening was a slow process for five-year-old Larry Kuntz. It came in stages, each stage bringing a new universe of agony with it. Something was wrong with his vision. It was dim and blurry. His numb and cold fingers worked clumsily around his swollen and bloody face. Shivering uncontrollably, he could feel dried blood on his cheekbone and in his hair. There was also a terrible throbbing in his head. Struggling to keep his eyes open in the dim light, Larry slowly realized he was in the corner of the backseat of his parents' car.

Beside Larry, curled up on the floor, was his mother. Her face was puffy and swollen around her eyes, and the dark bruises were a sharp contrast to her now ashen skin. It was obvious to Larry that she had been badly beaten and something was terribly wrong. When he grabbed her hand, it was extremely cold and stiff, and when he cried out to his mama, she did not move at all. Larry was overcome with panic and fear as he hugged her and cried out to her, "Help me, mama. Please wake up. Why are you so cold?"

Confused and in extreme pain, the frightened little boy then turned his eyes to the pale body of his father, Mike, who was slumped slightly forward in the front seat of the car. Larry grabbed and shook his father and called out to him, "Papa, Papa, something is wrong with Mama." When his papa gave no response, he knew his father was dead. Larry now saw the blood that had clung to the pale, cold skin of his father's face. Screaming in fear, Larry was unable to arouse his mother or father. As he tried to remember what had happened, he began to realize that he was now alone in the world. His parents were gone, and if he wanted to save himself, it was going to be up to him to do it. Forcing himself to look around, he started to think about escaping the car.

Larry's head constantly pounded, and he continued to weep and cry out to his parents. They seemed oddly at peace in their repose. It seemed to Larry that they were sleeping. Larry cried out for help again, hugging the bodies of his parents, hoping someone would hear his pleas for help.

The cold was just too intense. In the town of Billings, about 40 miles away, the morning low was 22 degrees, which did not reflect the wind chill factor. Larry knew he had to move or he would freeze to death.

He struggled to open the back door of the car. For a moment, the door wouldn't move, and then Larry remembered it opened the opposite way of the car's front doors. His own pain and confusion at being alone now threatened to overwhelm him. His tiny hands were shaking uncontrollably as he pulled on the frigid door handle. He tried once again to get out of the car. This time, he pushed the forward part of the door out and back and it swung open.

As Larry stood to climb out of the backseat, he noticed that the windshield had a bullet hole in it. The glass on the driver's side window was shattered. For a moment, Larry thought his dad would be mad about that. Then he glanced at his dad's body and shoved the thought aside.

The wintry wind that whipped across the barren Montana plains caused eerie creaking sounds in the elevator. Taking in more of his surroundings, Larry realized that he was inside the grain elevator where he had played so many times before. That explained the dusty rich grain smell that hung in the air. Rubbing his arms to fight off the cold, he clutched his coat close to him as he tried to make out details in the dim interior on this frigid November morning. As there was very little natural light on that gray morning and very few windows, it was difficult to find his way around. Larry found and checked the doors that led to the main street, but they were latched from the outside. As he searched for a way out of the elevator, Larry continually worked his way back to the car, imploring his mama and papa to please help him and to be all right. But deep in his heart, he knew they would not be. He knew they would never again be all right.

Adding to Larry's confusion and fear was the constant throbbing in his head. It was a relentless pain that shot through him with every heartbeat. Once again he went back to the car and climbed back inside to check on his parents, hoping that this was all a terrible nightmare from which they would awaken. They could then all go home, and everything would be as it was.

He couldn't recall what had happened to him, or the vicious beating he had endured at the hands of Robideau. He did remember Frank shooting his mama and papa. Larry knew that he needed to get help and, to do so, he would have to figure out how to get out of the grain elevator. He had checked the doors already and there were no windows he could use. The opening at the top of the elevator was over 60 feet off the ground, and would not help. There had to be another way out. Larry forced himself to think.

Over the months that his father had worked at the elevator, Larry had explored nearly every nook and cranny of the interior of this building while his papa worked. Larry remembered watching intently as Mike would open a door from the inside to access the wooden platform where the sacks of grain were loaded onto the railroad cars. That would be his way out.

The latch for the door was hidden in the shadows. It was high up on the wall, but Larry knew about where to look for it. The thin light of the morning coming in the narrow windows helped him get his bearings. He would escape this familiar playground that had now become his prison.

Using his small hands, Larry searched the walls for the handle that he knew would lead to a way out. At first, he could not find the latch. It had to be here! At last he came across the hook and latch that he had watched his papa open so many times before. He struggled to lift the heavy hook that secured the loading door blocking his exit. Larry gathered his strength, and with a great effort, he was able to unlatch the hook and slide open the large door.

Mike Visser slowly walked to work through a light dusting of snow from his home and across the only main street of Wheat Basin on Saturday morning of November 27, 1937. He was ready to start another day at his general store. He loved the business, but wondered how long he could keep it going. The town was shrinking, and soon there would be too few customers for him to make any profit. Mike set about getting ready to open for business. While he was sweeping the floor and anticipating the start of another uneventful day, a local farmer named Frank Robideau came in to visit. Lately there seemed to be more visitors than paying customers, Mike thought. Before Mike could complete this thought, in walked Hubert King, another local resident.

"Hey Mike, did you see those two hitchhikers that were in town last night?" Frank asked.

"No," said Mike, "I went to bed early, at about 7:30."

"Well, they came over to my house to ask for something to eat, but damned if I was going to give them anything," Frank said. "I told them to start walking toward Columbus and then get on the main highway. One was a man and the other a woman dressed in men's clothes, and they sure looked desperate."

The cold wind confronted Larry as he stood in the now open doorway of the grain elevator's loading dock. Stumbling out onto the wooden platform, Larry looked down to a drop of about five feet to the ground. He felt torn between staying with his mama and papa, or getting help for them and himself. Gathering his courage, Larry closed his eyes and jumped, feeling as though he was in a free fall. The jolt as Larry hit the cold hard ground drove him to his hands and knees. The sting of gravel on his skin was just one more pain to add to his multiple injuries. Larry was very weak from loss of blood, and he was in a world of extreme pain from the terrible beating he had endured the night before. Forcing himself to stand upright, his thoughts turned to his survival and getting help.

Larry shook all over as he put one foot in front of the other. He realized that he was on the railroad tracks and needed to cross them. Climbing down the elevated embankment, the little boy started to stumble in the direction of the main road. He was heading toward the general store. This was the store that he and his mother went to on shopping days. Mr. Visser would always give him a treat. Briefly, he wondered if he would get a treat today. Larry knew the kind store owner would be able to help him.

Larry was in serious trouble. Icy cold wind, the overwhelming pain of his injuries, loss of blood, and fatigue all made him just want to sit and rest for a while on the cold ground. The general store was only about four hundred yards from the elevator, but for the little boy, it may as well have been ten miles. Once on the main road, Larry could see his house, but with a pang of near panic, he could also see the house of Frank Robideau. Frank might spot him!

As quickly as he could, Larry slid down into the ditch that ran along the side of the road, collecting a new set of scrapes and cuts on his way down. He was determined to survive. He gathered his courage and crawled on hands and knees until he was well past the Robideau home. Once he felt he was safe, Larry climbed back up onto the road and continued his torturous journey to the store.

Awakening on the road, he could feel the cold of the frozen ground burning his cheek. The last thing Larry remembered was stumbling along the road. He realized that he had fainted. Slowly, he forced his broken body to stand and move toward the store again. Once more, he awoke to find himself lying on the ground. It would be so easy to just give up and rest there. He did not feel the cold as much anymore. He was not shivering now. It was just too tiring. Realizing the store was now close by, he made one last gallant effort to complete his mission.

Larry finally reached the general store about 9 a.m. He could not get his hands to open and grasp the door. As he fumbled with the handle on the front door, Mike Visser ran to open it. He was shocked to find a bedraggled, blood-soaked, and seriously injured young boy there. Mike let out a yell of surprise and quickly helped Larry inside.

When Frank Robideau saw Larry, he felt his heart sink. He was in real danger. His mind raced and he quickly thought to shout, "Oh my god, it's the Kuntz kid!" Before Larry had a chance to speak, Frank abruptly added, "What happened? Did a dog bite you?"

Mike and the others in the store didn't think anything of Frank's forceful question. A dog might have attacked Larry. He was dazed, covered in blood, and seemed to be in shock. Mr. Visser asked one of the men in the store, Hubert King of Molt, to take Larry home. Larry objected, quietly saying no one was home.

With downcast eyes, Larry took a deep breath and in a quiet dull voice said, "Someone killed my mama and papa last night." He drew a choking breath and continued, "they are over there," and pointed in the direction of the Occident Grain Elevator.

As Larry glanced around the room at the small group of men, his eyes locked on Frank's menacing glare. Larry froze. His worst fear was standing there, glaring at him. Here was the man who had killed

The hitchhikers, Mr. and Mrs. Hugh Downard, originally blamed by Robideau for the Kuntz murders. *(Courtesy Victor Murphy)*

his parents, now boldly lying, and standing in front of him. He fainted, falling into the arms of Mike Visser.

The Robideau home in Wheat Basin, Montana. Frank Robideau, his wife, May, and their three children lived in this home. Richard, one of the children, who was about the same age as Larry, became his best friend and playmate. May was expecting her fourth child in December 1937. Frieda and May became close enough in their friendship that May asked Frieda to be the midwife during the delivery of her baby. *(Courtesy Victor Murphy)*

Frank Robideau, 1891 – 1938.
(Courtesy Victor Murphy)

Chapter Three
The Investigation

At 9:15 a.m. on November 27, Sheriff Frank Murphy was in his office in Columbus, Montana, catching up on a desktop full of paperwork when the loud ringing of his phone interrupted him. Frank was good with people, so he had jumped at the chance to be the undersheriff. He loved the work, and the following year he ran for the position of sheriff for Stillwater County. Frank was very popular with the people in the area and was elected with ease. There was an increase in salary and a nice home that went along with this position. Frank was determined to do a good job for all of the people in the county.

The Stillwater County Courthouse (on the right) with the county jail located on the back side. On the left is the sheriff's residence where Murphy and his family resided. (*Hattenburg photo*)

Murphy answered the phone, and knew instantly from Mike Visser's tone that any hopes for a quiet day were dashed. Visser was calling from his general store in Wheat Basin, twenty-six miles away. He was frantic and a little scared. He told the sheriff that he had a five-year-old boy in his store who had been severely beaten. Before the little boy had passed out he told Visser and two other customers at the store that his mama and papa were dead in the elevator, and pointed to the Occident Grain Elevator where his papa, Mike Kuntz, was the manager. Visser informed the sheriff that he had already called Dr. William Smith for medical help, but was sure they would need Murphy's assistance as well. From the amount of blood on the boy, he had no cause to doubt the boy's assertions.

Visser also informed the sheriff that a few men who had been in the store were now on their way to check out the scene at the elevator and would meet the sheriff at the store when he and the doctor arrived. Murphy wasted no time in summoning his undersheriff, Jack S. Benjamin, who lived only a few blocks from the courthouse and county jail. Benjamin told the sheriff he could be at the office in just a few minutes and would go to Wheat Basin with him. The sheriff then hurriedly walked from the jail to his house next door. As he waited for Benjamin, he informed his wife, Judith, of the shocking phone call that he had just received and told her he would most likely be gone for the rest of the day. Murphy returned to the office as Benjamin drove up, and the two of them immediately headed out to Wheat Basin in Murphy's Plymouth coupe.

As they made the best possible speed on the terrible road that gray Saturday morning, they both vowed silently to bring a quick resolution to this horrendous crime. To murder another man was bad enough, but to kill his wife and savagely beat a young boy made this case personal to both men.

The drive from Columbus to Wheat Basin took about an hour. Murphy used the time to bring Benjamin up to speed on what Mike Visser had related to him in his phone call. They discussed the fact that in all their years of law enforcement, neither one of them had investigated a crime of this type.

As they entered the town of Wheat Basin, the general store was the first stop they made in order to check on the little boy and talk to Mike Visser and anyone else that might be there. As the officers entered, they saw that the doctor had arrived and was starting to examine Larry. Murphy took charge of the scene and asked the men gathered around the injured little boy to step away and give Dr. Smith some room. He let them all know he would need a full account from each of them regarding what had transpired that morning.

Frank Robideau spoke up first and told him that about 9:00 a.m. he and Mike Visser were visiting when they heard the little Kuntz boy at the door. Upon seeing him at the door, Visser had run over and helped him inside. According to Mike Visser, his entire head was a mass of dried blood and his eyes were noticeably blackened.

Robideau said he had asked Larry if a dog had attacked him. The boy replied, "Someone killed my mama and papa last night and they are over there," as he pointed in the direction of the grain elevator.

Robideau told how the little boy then suddenly passed out and Hubert King quickly wrapped blankets around his shivering body. Mike Visser then gently picked him up and placed him in the rocking chair next to the stove, and immediately proceeded to call for the doctor and the sheriff.

View toward the rear of the Kuntz vehicle. Notice Mike's small office on the right side of the photo. The car was parked on the scales used for weighing trucks loaded with grain. *(Photo by Victor Murphy, courtesy Museum of the Beartooths)*

Frank then quickly added that a few minutes later, he noticed that Larry seemed to have regained consciousness so he went over to him and asked if it was the hitchhikers that did it and Larry had replied, "Yes, hitchhikers," and passed out again.

Robideau also told the officers that the men in the store at the time had decided to investigate the grain elevator. Mike Visser had offered to stay with Larry and went about cleaning the boy's blood-soaked face with a damp cloth. As Robideau and Hubert King were running down the street, Ira Reams, the mail carrier from Billings, who was on his way to his delivery at the general store, and Louis Paulson, another Wheat Basin farmer, asked them what their hurry was.

King briefly shared with Reams and Paulson the story the Kuntz boy had told them and that they were on their way to check it out. The two of them joined with Frank and Hubert and the quartet continued to the Occident Grain Elevator. The first thing they noticed was a handwritten sign on the door that read, "WE ARE CLOSED TODAY."

Hubert King warned the group not to touch anything that the sheriff might need as evidence. Leaving the sign hanging on the door, Ira Reams carefully unlatched then opened the elevator door and was the first to enter the building, followed by the other three men. They saw that Mike Kuntz's car was parked on the scales used to weigh the grain trucks. They were rushing, hoping against hope that Mike and Frieda Kuntz might still be alive. However, even in the dim light of the interior, they could clearly see that the Kuntzes were beyond any help.

The scene they encountered was horrifying. The men were able to see the blood on the running boards of the car, and as they came closer, they could see the bodies of Mike and Frieda inside the vehicle. The fatal wounds inflicted on them were clearly visible. Ira Reams could see that Mr. Kuntz was positioned just to the right of the steering wheel with his head leaning back against the front seat, and Mrs. Kuntz was lying in the back of the car on the floor with her arm thrown over the front seat.

The four men had looked at each other with disbelief in the realization that the poor little boy must have spent the entire night in the car with the bodies of his parents. Visibly shaken, the men abruptly exited from the ghastly scene and then shut the elevator door, hoping to protect the crime scene for the sheriff. Frank, Louis, and Hubert then proceeded to return to the general store.

Police vehicles parked outside the Occident Grain Elevator on November 27, 1937. The officers were inside investigating the Kuntz murders. *(Photo by Victor Murphy, courtesy Museum of the Beartooths)*

Ira Reams was the only mail carrier for the area, so he needed to continue his route. He slowly walked away from the other men as the surreal death scene they had just witnessed kept flashing through his mind. Ira found it very difficult to understand how anyone could commit such a horrible, cold-blooded crime.

Sheriff Murphy and Undersheriff Jack Benjamin asked Robideau to tell them about the hitchhikers that Visser said Robideau had seen the night before. Frank described them as a man and woman. The man was about 40 years old, 5 feet 8 inches tall with a heavy build and sandy hair. The woman looked to be about 10 years younger, had a slender build and dark complexion. She was wearing men's clothing, and they were both dressed shabbily. He said the couple had come to his door at about 5 p.m. Friday evening begging for food. According to Frank, they said that they were trying to get to Billings to find work. Nodding, the sheriff said he was familiar with the couple and knew where they were staying, and he would go to talk with them after he checked on the Kuntzes. Murphy then thanked Frank for giving him a potentially important lead in the case.

After he finished an initial examination of Larry, Dr. Smith informed the sheriff the young boy was in serious but stable condition, with a deep laceration by his right eye and a couple of gashes that had opened his scalp. However, the good news was that the bleeding had stopped. He also said Larry would need to be transported to the Stillwater County Hospital in Columbus for treatment and further observation. Dr. Smith then asked Sheriff Murphy if there was anything else he would need from him.

Murphy responded by inquiring if it would be alright to leave Larry for a short period of time in order for Smith to accompany them to the grain elevator to check on the status of the Kuntzes. Dr. Smith said he thought Larry's condition wouldn't change dramatically in the next few hours, and even though he was in a deep sleep, he had a fairly normal pulse and breathing pattern. The fact that he had been walking and able to converse with the men when he entered the store also bode well for his long-term outlook. If he had been in the cold much longer, he probably would have died.

Sheriff Murphy, Undersheriff Benjamin, and Dr. Smith drove the short distance to the Occident Grain Elevator. As they entered the elevator,

Front view of the Kuntz car. Frieda's arm is draped over the front seat. Also, Mike's body was no longer behind the steering wheel. It had been moved by Robideau to the center of the front seat. The bullet hole in the lower left of the windshield had exited Frieda's body. *(Photo by Victor Murphy, courtesy Museum of the Beartooths)*

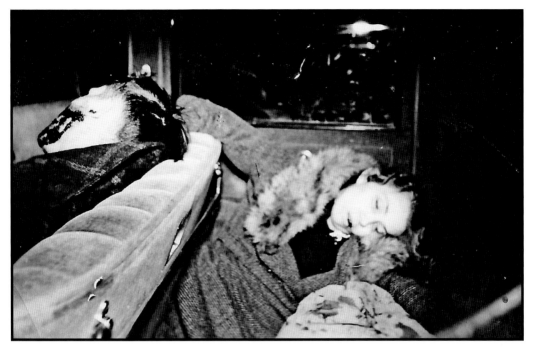

The bodies of Mike and Frieda, as found by the officers and the doctor on November 27. The slain couple died together on their eighth wedding anniversary. *(Photo by Victor Murphy, courtesy Museum of the Beartooths)*

they saw the note, "WE ARE CLOSED TODAY," hanging on the door. If the Kuntzes were dead inside, it was unlikely they had written the sign. The sheriff wondered who had. Murphy would have his son Victor photograph the sign along with the rest of the evidence. He then opened the door, and as the rays from the sun were now well above the horizon, illuminating the interior of the elevator, they could clearly see the car sitting on the scales.

Approaching the vehicle, they observed a bullet hole in the windshield, as well as the driver's side window, and also that the running boards were covered with blood. Peering through the window, Murphy saw that the body of Mike Kuntz was in the front seat, with his face covered in blood. He had been shot in the head. From the blood splatter, they figured the shot had been at very close range. Frieda Kuntz was in a half-kneeling position on the rear floor with one arm draped over the front seat. The officers carefully opened the left rear door, where it seemed that there was the least amount of evidence to disturb. Dr. Smith entered the back seat in order to check on the unfortunate couple, and confirmed the earlier presumptions of their deaths. In a quick observation, he noted that Mike had been shot in the back of the head and Frieda had been shot in the left chest. Her face bore the marks of a beating. There was also evidence of a struggle that had preceded her death, with blood on her left temple as well as on the left side of her mouth. There were also powder burns on her coat, where the gun had been fired at very close range.

After looking over the scene, Dr. Smith and the officers theorized that Mike Kuntz had been shot first, the bullet entering just behind the right ear, exiting below the left lower ear and shattering the side window. From the angle of the wound, the killer would have been sitting in the back seat directly behind Mike. Frieda, who had apparently been riding in the front passenger side, must have lunged over the seat and tried to fight with the killer, which would explain the bruises on her face. The officers also discovered that three other bullets had been fired. One bullet exited through the roof, one lodged in the side pocket on the passenger side, and the third lodged in the support beam of the windshield. Assuming those bullets were fired during the struggle between Frieda and the killer, the fifth bullet, the last one fired, went through Frieda's heart, exiting through her back and piercing the windshield instantly killing her.

Most people typically did not put a bullet in the first chamber of their guns. Without this measure, an accidental discharge was almost a certainty at some point. This meant the killer was probably out of bullets after firing five shots. This would explain why little Larry was so severely beaten and then left for dead rather than being shot along with his parents.

Even though Mike and Frieda had bled heavily from the wounds they suffered, the officers noticed that there were no traces of blood on the floor of the elevator beneath the car. Murphy and Benjamin did a quick search, but couldn't find any glass from the car's broken windows and, despite a fairly thorough search, no gun was found in the car.

"This was not the murder scene," concluded Murphy. The doctor pointed out that it also appeared that Mike's body had been tampered with. The sheriff agreed. The killer had most likely moved to the front seat and pushed Mike over just enough to get in behind the wheel and drive the car to that location. When he arrived at the elevator, the killer then drove the car inside, closed the door behind him, and latched it from the outside. Upon leaving, the sign was put up to keep anyone from entering the elevator and finding the car with the bodies of the Kuntz family inside.

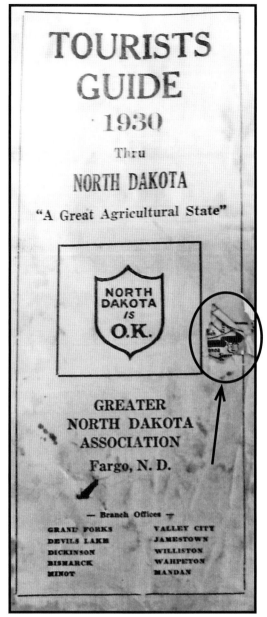

One of the stray bullets fired by Robideau went into the side pocket of the car. When Val Kuntz took the car back to North Dakota, he found a road map in that side pocket with a bullet hole in it. *(Courtesy Richard Kuntz, Hattenburg photo)*

Sheriff Frank Murphy of Stillwater County, Montana. *(Photo by Victor Murphy, courtesy Museum of the Beartooths)*

Undersheriff Jack Benjamin. *(Photo by Victor Murphy, courtesy Museum of the Beartooths)*

The front view of the car, after the bodies had been removed. Officers fingerprinted the car and searched it for evidence in hopes of finding the couple's killer. *(Photo by Victor Murphy, courtesy Museum of the Beartooths)*

Knowing the crime scene needed to be processed before the bodies could be taken to the coroner's office, Murphy used the phone on Mike's desk to call Sheriff Dan Stephenson of the Yellowstone County Sheriff's Department in Billings. Stephenson was aghast at the news of the double homicide and said he would send Deputy Albert Jansen, a fingerprinting expert, on his way directly to Wheat Basin.

Two other officers from Billings Township were also being sent out to assist in the investigation. Constables Albert Thomas and Earl Wilson were more than anxious to help solve this rare and heinous crime. Murphy asked them to meet him in Columbus and, on their way, to watch for the hitchhikers Robideau had described. As Robideau had said they were going in the direction of Billings to look for work, they might see them on the road.

Murphy next contacted his son Victor. Murphy wanted Victor to bring his camera and take photos of the car, and the bodies of Mike and Frieda, also of any other evidence, including the sign on the door. When he was through with his photographs and Deputy Jansen finished fingerprinting, the bodies were to be transported to the coroner and undertaker, O.

R. Ray McColley, in Columbus. The deputies were to bring any evidence they found back to the sheriff's office.

Once again, Murphy made sure the elevator was closed and secured. He suspected there were still things to be learned there, and he wanted to preserve any potential evidence and prevent any accidental tampering by curious onlookers. As the officers left the elevator, they noted two major mistakes the killer had made so far. The most obvious one was mistakenly letting Larry live. They were sure the killer did not intend for the little boy to survive. After his brutal beating, they were sure the killer presumed he was dead. This left the possibility that he would eventually be able to identify the assailant. The second mistake was the note, which was clearly written by the killer. If they could find out who wrote that note, they would have the murderer.

The officers and Dr. Smith returned to the general store. Larry remained in an undisturbed sleep. Undersheriff Benjamin went back out to the car to get blankets from the trunk and made a bed on the back seat of the doctor's car for the injured child. Smith told Sheriff Murphy that it

The shattered glass on the driver's side window was the result of the bullet that exited Mike Kuntz's body when he was shot. Notice the blood running down the lower part of the window. *(Photo by Victor Murphy, courtesy Museum of the Beartooths)*

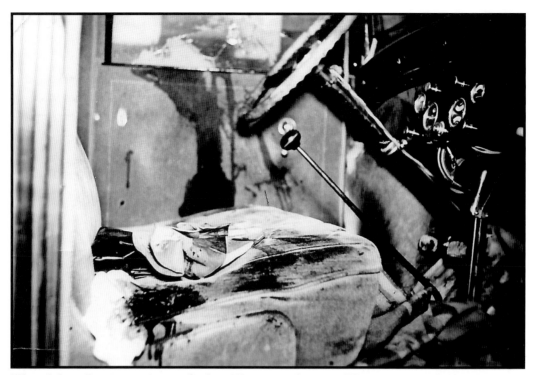

The bloody interior of the Kuntzes' car. There was blood running down the side of the door and a bullet-shattered window on the driver's side. Frieda's pocketbook is on the seat. *(Photo by Victor Murphy, courtesy Museum of the Beartooths)*

was fortunate the killer had parked the car in the elevator out of the direct blast of the frigid, cold-night air. It was probably at least 10 degrees warmer in the elevator than it was outside, and he felt that this saved Larry from hypothermia and certain death. Murphy agreed. He gently carried Larry outside to the car and settled him in the back seat. Driving carefully, Dr. Smith then started his journey to the Stillwater County Hospital in Columbus.

With Larry on his way to receiving the medical treatment he needed, Sheriff Murphy had to make an unpleasant phone call. After finding out from Mr. Visser that the Kuntzes had come from Richardton, North Dakota, he used the phone in the general store and asked the operator to connect him with the Dickinson's Sheriff's Office. Murphy explained to the sheriff the circumstances of the deaths of Mike and Frieda, and described the injuries Larry had suffered. Sheriff Gerlick was shocked. He knew the Kuntz and Hammerchmidt (Frieda's maiden name) families, and he had liked Mike a lot. He promised to give them the tragic news and relay the latest on Larry's condition immediately.

Upon receiving the unbelievable news from his family in Richardton, Mike's brother Henry Kuntz of Missoula, Montana, made plans to leave on Sunday for Columbus. He would handle the arrangements needed to transport Mike and Frieda back to North Dakota for burial. Frieda's sister Genevieve Hammerschmidt would go stay with Larry while he recovered in the hospital, and bring him back to Richardton to live after recovering from his injuries. Another brother of Mike's, Val Kuntz, would accompany Genevieve by train the next day and help Henry during this extremely difficult time for the families of Mike and Frieda.

With that task completed, Murphy continued his investigation. He knew that the sooner he could collect the necessary evidence, the better chance he would have of solving this crime. The officers set out to interview the townspeople and farmers that lived around the Wheat Basin area.

Their first point of emphasis was whether any strangers had been seen in the area, or if anyone had been acting suspiciously. The officers knew this was probably not a random killing and that there must be a motive. During their interviews, they found that Mike and Frieda were well-liked and were quite popular. No one could imagine how anyone could do something so horrific to this family. Several of the residents were afraid of being a target of the killer still on the loose. This small community had never witnessed such an unnerving event, and it left many of them in fear.

The former grain elevator manager, Emil Melby, told the sheriff that he had warned Mike Kuntz that much of the grain was encumbered. Melby said he had advised Mike when he took over as the manager of the elevator, he needed to be sure that there were no liens against any of the wheat before writing checks for payment. Many of the farmers had already borrowed against the grain that was in storage. Some of the farmers were getting desperate, since there had been three consecutive years of poor crops due to a lack of rain and the plague of grasshoppers and crickets. Desperate men do desperate things.

All of the individuals that Murphy and Benjamin interviewed were able to account for their whereabouts on the night of the murders, except Frank Robideau. Frank said he had been home alone doing some work around his house. His wife, May, and their three children had spent Thanksgiving with her sister's family, the Ed Meyers, out near Columbus. Frank said he was going to go pick them up on Saturday evening.

It appeared the last person to have seen the Kuntzes alive, besides the killer, was Ted Lutgen, a friend who had seen Mike the previous afternoon and had invited Mike and Frieda to play cards at their home that night. It was the Kuntzes eighth wedding anniversary, and Ted and his wife thought a card party would be a fun way for all of them to celebrate the occasion. He told the sheriff that, when they didn't show up, he and his wife figured maybe Mike had to go to Columbus or Billings on business. Ted could not understand why Mike had not let them know that they would not be coming over. Murphy explained to Ted, according to the evidence he had gathered so far, the murders most likely happened not long after Mike arrived home from work, since he had the family with him and he was still dressed in his work clothes.

The only person who claimed to have seen anyone suspicious was Frank Robideau, who re-emphasized to Murphy that he had two hitchhikers come to his door begging for food. Frank repeated his story that he told them he had no food to give them and sent the couple on their way. Perhaps, Frank speculated, the hitchhikers had stopped Mike while he was driving down the road and got a ride with him. Maybe after a short distance, they forced Mike to pull over and killed him and his wife Frieda, then beat the boy. Sheriff Murphy agreed it was a definite possibility, which he would pursue.

With the interviews in town complete, Sheriff Murphy and Undersheriff Benjamin went to the small home where the Kuntz family had lived. It was a very short distance from the elevator, and Murphy felt sure something had happened there. Entering the house, they found firm evidence the family had left suddenly. They had not planned to go. The kitchen and dining areas had food and dishes still sitting out on the table. Frieda had the rest of the house in perfect order, and a person who was as organized as she would not have left the kitchen and dining area unkempt, unless she was compelled to leave in a hurry. She certainly would not have left food and dinner dishes on the table in order to get to a card party. The officers pondered why the family had departed in such haste. What would have caused them to leave their home and drive off into the night?

After leaving the Kuntz residence, Murphy called the Stillwater County Hospital from Mike Visser's store to check on the condition of little Larry. The doctor informed him that the boy had received a concussion and was still unable to be interviewed. He was only semiconscious and in no shape to answer questions. The doctor also told the officer that it looked like Larry would possibly be able to talk to him later in the day or that evening. Dr. Smith added that when changing the bandage on Larry's head he had found some potential evidence. He had found a small piece of wood in the wound, which he was saving for the sheriff.

Knowing that Officers Thomas and Wilson were on the way to Columbus from Billings, Benjamin and Murphy left the general store and headed back to Columbus. They had hopes of intercepting the hitchhikers if the other officers did not happen to come upon them first. The two lawmen had seen tire tracks leading from the Kuntz home going in the direction of Columbus. With the knowledge of the role the vehicle had played in the crime and now in full daylight, they drove slowly and carefully, studying the tire tracks on the way back.

While driving to Columbus, the officers decided to stop by the McKeehan farmhouse, which was next to the road, thinking they might have seen something. The interview with Bess McKeehan proved to be quite interesting. She said the Kuntz car drove by her home around 7 p.m. Friday evening going toward Columbus. A short time later, Bess heard the sound of a car and looked out to see the Kuntz car returning in the direction of Wheat Basin. When asked how she could be sure it was the Kuntz car, Bess said their vehicle was different from any other in town and was easily recognized. It was the only Chevy of its kind. Sheriff Murphy thanked Bess and told her the information was a tremendous help.

Continuing on their way, Murphy and Benjamin came near a building known as the "Stone" schoolhouse. This small building was about ten miles out of Wheat Basin. There they found what appeared to be the crime scene. There were two large pools of blood on the road. Near the blood they found shattered glass from the car windows. They also noticed the tracks they had been following indicated that the car had been turned around just past this point. With all of these details, Murphy and Benjamin felt that this was definitely the spot where the murders occurred.

The two officers decided investigating that lead was their next priority. They continued their drive toward a shack on a nearby farmer's property. They had information that this was where the hitchhiker couple was staying.

Before reaching the shack, they saw two individuals hitchhiking on the road. In the early afternoon sun, the men could see the couple matched the description of the alleged murder suspects. Not wanting to alarm them, Murphy gradually slowed down, pulled the car over and identified himself and Benjamin as law officers. When the sheriff asked the couple where they were headed, the man said that they were on their way to Columbus to look for work. Murphy said that he was going in the same direction and would give them a ride.

The traveling couple glanced at each other with a relieved look and gladly got into the car. Safe in the car, they could be warm and rest their tired legs. After driving about a mile, Benjamin turned around to face them. Carefully watching their reaction, he told them of the murders that had taken place in Wheat Basin the previous evening. He also told the couple that an individual who placed them in the area at the time of the killings had identified them. The couple was shocked at the news and immediately denied any knowledge of the crime. Benjamin noted their reaction and told the couple they were under arrest. In Columbus, they would be taken to the county jail for questioning. In an ironic turn of events, the shocked couple had gone from feeling safe and warm in Murphy's backseat to becoming suspects for a double murder.

Arriving in Columbus, Murphy met Constables Wilson and Thomas from Billings at the jail, and let them know that he had picked up the hitch-hikers who were now ready for questioning. The officers were asked to find Frank Robideau when they arrived in Wheat Basin and inform him the hitchhikers were in custody. They would need Frank to come to Columbus to make a positive identification of the couple at the courthouse. Then the sheriff brought Thomas and Wilson up to date on the information that they had collected so far. He instructed them to go out to Wheat Basin and to be meticulous in their examination of the recent records in Mike Kuntz's elevator office. They were to look through all of his personal and business effects, checking especially for any records of payments or collections that may look suspicious. They were also told that Deputy Albert Jansen of the Yellowstone County Sheriff's Department in Billings had already been sent to Wheat Basin to recover any fingerprints from the car, and they were to work with him in processing the crime scene.

Murphy, Benjamin, and the suspects then went to the office of County Attorney P. R. Pat Heily. The trio questioned the couple separately and at great length. The sheriff and the county attorney both asked where the couple had been the night before and tried to find out if there was anyone who could verify their story. The couple gave their names as Mr. Hugh Downard, age 40, and Mrs. Downard, age 28. They came from the state of Kentucky and were traveling in search of food, shelter, and work. Both Downards emphatically stated they had not been in Wheat Basin on Friday evening. Mr. Downard explained in great detail where they were at the approximate time the killings had occurred. Downard said he had walked to the home of Ross Lacey to ask for flour and syrup, as they had no food to eat and no money with which to purchase any. His wife decided to remain at their cabin rather than accompany her husband, as it was extremely cold that evening. When Hugh Downard arrived at the Lacey residence, he was invited in to have some dinner. He explained that his wife was waiting for him at their cabin and he didn't want to leave her alone very long, so declined the invitation. Downard said Mr. Lacey nodded in agreement, gave him flour and syrup, as well as a ride back to the shack where they were staying at the old homestead of Billy Cole near Hensly Creek. There they were waiting for work with the Harris Cattle Company.

Undersheriff Benjamin faced the press late Saturday afternoon. He told the gathered reporters they had apprehended a man and his wife in the double slaying of Mike and Frieda Kuntz, and they were being questioned at the Stillwater County Jail. The murders and the arrest of the Downards was big news. It made headlines in all the papers around the area and as far away as Spokane, Washington, by the next morning.

P. R. Heily continued to question the Downards. They were unwavering in explaining where they were and what they were doing the previous evening. Privately, Murphy, Benjamin, and Heily were becoming increasingly convinced the Downards were telling the truth. Their actions in gladly greeting the sheriff's offer of a ride did not hint at any sort of a guilty conscience. The two lawmen had seen lots of good liars, but the couple's reaction to the news of the murders was shock, not fear. Their story was too detailed and consistent for them to be the killers. These people were innocent.

Still, Murphy needed to see if Larry Kuntz or Frank Robideau could positively identify the Downards. Hoping Larry was awake, he called the hospital and spoke with the nurse in charge of Larry's care. Murphy asked if she felt that the little boy would be alert enough to possibly identify the suspects they had in custody. The nurse said that the boy was still groggy. However, they could see how he would respond to questions. She cautioned Murphy be as quick as possible.

Hearing the potentially good news, the officers quickly traveled the three and a half blocks to the hospital with the Downards in custody. Murphy wanted to check on Larry first and see if he was ready to identify the Downards. Benjamin and the couple waited in the hallway.

As the sheriff entered Larry's hospital room, he was extremely surprised to see that Frank Robideau was there speaking in what seemed to be a low, menacing tone to the child. The sheriff was unable to hear what Frank was saying to the frightened young boy, although it seemed to Murphy that whatever he said to Larry had left him visibly shaken.

Murphy was angry that Robideau seemed to be upsetting Larry and demanded to know why he was at the hospital. He had told Robideau they would meet in the sheriff's office at the courthouse. Robideau replied that he was worried about his son's favorite playmate and had stopped by to check on the condition of the little boy on his way to meet up with Murphy.

The sheriff's instincts told him that there were ulterior motives to this visit. The boy was too frightened. Robideau was too tense. Something else was going on. Murphy's first priority was making Larry feel safe. He ordered Robideau to back away from the young boy's hospital bed and stand by the wall. As Robideau slowly moved back, Murphy could not help noticing that he continued to keep a steady gaze on Larry and had a threatening look on his face. The sheriff then had Benjamin bring the Downards into the room and stand at the foot of Larry's bed. Murphy asked Larry if he recognized the couple as the hitchhikers that his dad had given a ride to on the night of the murders. After glancing over at Robideau, he then looked at the couple and nervously said the man looked familiar, but not the woman.

Frank Robideau was then asked if he could positively identify the couple as the ones that had come to his door on the evening the murders took place. In an intimidating manner, Robideau took a step toward them and said he was positive that they were the man and woman who had been at his home begging for food.

Reacting in disbelief, Hugh Downard responded by angrily saying, "How dare you lie about us. We have never been to your home and we certainly were not there Friday night."

Hearing the Downards' denial, Robideau got extremely upset and insisted that they were lying and that they had indeed been to his house. Sheriff Murphy told Robideau to calm down and said he was going to keep the Downards in custody until he could confirm their alibi.

Before Murphy and Benjamin left the hospital room to return the Downards to the county jail, the sheriff demanded that Robideau also leave the room to allow Larry to get his much-needed rest. He angrily walked out ahead of the small group and said he was on his way to pick up his wife and children anyway.

The sheriff then led the way down the hall, and as they approached the nurse in charge of Larry, Murphy stopped. He asked that no one be allowed to visit Larry without his permission until the little boy's Aunt Genevieve arrived to stay with him. The nurse agreed, and the group continued to the jail.

After placing the Downards in a jail cell, Murphy received a call from Coroner O. R. Ray McColley. The man was anxious to share his findings from his examination of Mike and Frieda Kuntz. He said the Kuntzes had been dead approximately 15 hours when they were found in the elevator, which would put the time of their death between 6 p.m. and 7 p.m. the previous night. He also told the sheriff that he had found $13 ($200 in today's money value) in Mike Kuntz's pocket. A few more dollars were found in Frieda's purse, so robbery was not likely the motive for the murders. McColley also confirmed that the bullets used to kill the Kuntzes were fired from a .38 caliber pistol.

At the conclusion of the phone call, the officers got into the sheriff's car for the long drive to the home of Ross Lacey on the Harris Ranch. While on their way there, Murphy told Benjamin what the coroner had said. The men talked over the case and agreed that it didn't make any sense for the money to still be with the Kuntzes. If the Downards had been so desperate to rob and kill the Kuntz family, why didn't they take their money and leave town? Benjamin agreed and added that it made even less sense for them to have driven the car back to the elevator. The Downards could have just left the bodies at the murder scene and driven the vehicle a long distance away before anyone was even aware of the killings.

When they reached the home of Ross Lacey, foreman of the Harris Cattle Company, Murphy and Benjamin explained to him that they were following up on a potential alibi for his neighbors, the Downards. Murphy asked if Lacey had seen the couple on the night of the murders. Mr. Lacey said that Hugh Downard had indeed been to his home Friday night at around 5 o'clock, asking for syrup and flour. Ross also said he had felt bad for their situation, and had invited Hugh in to warm up and have some dinner. Declining the invitation, Downard had explained that he could not stay to eat because his wife was waiting for him at their cabin, as it was too cold for her to be out. Ross added that Downard had remained at the Lacey home long enough to have been seen by Ben Woltermann and Jack McClure, who were also employees at the Harris ranch. Undersheriff Benjamin located the two ranch hands, and they also confirmed seeing Downard on Friday evening after 5 o'clock.

On the drive back to Columbus, the two officers concluded that the Downard's alibi was airtight. Reviewing the information they had gathered so far, they also concluded that the murderer must be someone who knew the Kuntzes. Some of the locals who were interviewed by the officers had told them, "When the elevator scales were not in use, Mike would keep his car parked there to protect it from the elements." They also pointed out that his house was nearby, and he could walk home in a matter of minutes. A stranger would have no reason to have known this information. The officers also went back over the fact that robbery was apparently not a motive. They reasoned the killing must have resulted over a personal confrontation of some kind.

When they arrived at the Stillwater County Jail in Columbus, Murphy informed the Downards that Ross Lacey as well as two other ranch hands confirmed their alibi. He also explained to them, after their arrest, he had sent their fingerprints by airmail to the Federal Bureau of Investigation of the Department of Justice. They would need to remain in jail until they received a report from government authorities, but they would be released as soon as they were cleared of any other possible crimes.

Murphy's wife, Judith, brought one of her savory southern-style dinners over to the jail to feed the Downards. She was an excellent cook, and provided generous portions, which were welcomed by the hungry couple. Judith had a gracious manner, and between the meal and the reassurance that they were believed, the Downards began to relax for the first time since their arrest.

While Judith was there, Sheriff Murphy told her he was glad they were receiving a good home-cooked meal. The community was outraged at the murders, and he was glad for the chance to keep the Downards safe from any possible vigilantes until the killer was found. Benjamin and the other officers involved knew that Murphy probably could have released the Downards. They did not have the means to go anywhere, but the sheriff was doing what he could to protect them. Murphy was well-known for his kind and caring manner. It was no surprise that Sheriff Murphy would shelter and feed the couple he now knew were innocent of the terrible crime.

While Murphy and Benjamin were questioning the Downards, Albert Jansen took fingerprints from the car. With the help of the other officers, he examined the elevator for more evidence. They discovered an open checkbook with the check register of the Occident Grain Company on Mike Kuntz's desk. They found check stubs indicating that six checks had been written on Friday, November 26. Five of them were made out in various amounts ranging from $10 to $20 with the sixth one in the amount of $675. In 2014 dollars that would be about $11,172. The register showed that they were written out to Mike Visser, Paul Schuman, Frank Robideau, and other Wheat Basin residents.

This was a new angle and plausible motive for murder. The officers immediately presented the check stubs to the residents, and asked if they were familiar with them. All of them stated that they had no knowledge of the checks, nor had they received any money from them. The one large check was made out to Frank Robideau. When the officers confronted him with it, he denied knowledge of the check and acted very agitated in his denial.

Later that evening, the officers who had been at the Wheat Basin elevator met with Murphy and Benjamin in Columbus to go over their findings. Along with the check stubs, they were also able to recover clear fingerprints from the car. Officer Jansen was now preparing to send them and the sign from the door to the Department of Justice for a possible match. The officers also shared the reactions of Robideau when they confronted him with the $675 check stub.

Robideau's name kept coming up. His reaction to the hitchhikers, his being at the hospital, his violent reaction to the checks, all began to look very suspicious. With this additional information, Sheriff Murphy decided to call and talk with Mike Visser, the Wheat Basin store owner. It was Visser who had initially contacted the sheriff Saturday morning. Murphy asked Visser who had actually heard Larry say it was the hitchhikers that killed the Kuntzes. He said that after Larry had collapsed and he had been settled into the rocking chair, Frank Robideau went over and talked to him in a low whisper. Visser was reluctant to say bad things about Robideau, but he did not like how he had asked Larry in a voice loud enough for every one to hear, "Who did this? Was it the hitchhikers?"

Visser said Frank then told the rest of the men in the store that Larry had said, "Yes, the hitchhikers." No one else had heard Larry's actual reply.

In his and Undersheriff Benjamin's interviews, Murphy recalled several of the townspeople had expressed that they felt Robideau was acting oddly in their daily encounters with him. Some of his neighbors even said they were afraid of him. They felt that he could not be trusted. The townspeople were worried about him. He became easily agitated and was always on edge. He was like a time bomb waiting to go off.

Clearly Robideau had been either badly mistaken, or he was lying when he attempted to throw suspicion on the two transients. His positive identification of them as the persons who called at his home at 5 o'clock Friday evening in search of something to eat did not ring true. The Downards had established a clear-cut alibi, which was iron-clad. They could not have been in two places at the same time. The Robideau house and the cabin were more than 13 miles apart. After a long evening of analyzing the evidence they had, the officers took a much-needed rest and planned to begin again early Sunday morning.

About the same time that all the officers gathered at the jailhouse office on Sunday morning, the hospital nurse was in Larry's room. While checking on him, she found the little boy awake and more alert. The nurse was ecstatic to see the improvement in his condition. When asked how he was feeling, he replied with some energy that he was much better. The little boy had become attached to his kind, loving nurse. She was cheerful and efficient and did not ask him difficult questions. He felt safe and secure in her presence. As she was changing his bandages, he abruptly said to her, "It was Mr. Robideau that killed my mama and papa."

The nurse, not knowing that the Downards had been cleared of any wrong doing, explained to Larry that it could not possibly be true because they had a man and a woman in jail who they thought were responsible for the killings. She had expected Larry to be glad of this news. Instead he got more upset. As Larry continued to insist that it was Robideau, the nurse said she would contact the sheriff right away and ask him to come to the hospital.

The nurse then called the sheriff's office to inform him that Larry Kuntz was now more aware of his surroundings and that he needed to talk about the murders. When Murphy received this message, he was excited. The sheriff felt that they might find out more details that would assist them in their investigation.

As Murphy drove the short distance to the Stillwater County Hospital his mind was racing. He was comforted with the knowledge that Larry's condition was improving. Larry's Aunt Genevieve would be arriving the next morning to stay with him until his recovery was complete. Larry would pull through. Thank heavens Mike Visser had acted so promptly to help Larry.

As he strode into the room, the sheriff's heart went out to the little boy who lay there. His head was wrapped in bandages, and he peered out at the world with blackened eyes. The small boy looked so fragile and so alone on the hospital bed. Seeing Larry in this condition made Murphy even more determined to track down the person responsible.

Larry saw the sheriff as he came in and motioned for him to come closer. Murphy approached the bedside and gently moved a stray lock of hair from Larry's face. As the big sheriff leaned closer to the small boy, Larry whispered in his ear, "It was Mr. Robideau that killed my mama and papa."

Boy Survives; Parents Killed

Five-year-old Larry Kuntz of Wheat Basin, Mont., is shown in a hospital at Columbus, where he is recovering from wounds inflicted by Frank Robideau, right who has confessed the murder of the child's parents. He said he shot them after a dispute over ownership of grain

Larry in the Stillwater County Hospital. He is pictured with the nurse who took care of him and contacted Sheriff Murphy regarding the identification of Frank Robideau as his parents' killer. The nurse's name is not known. *(Courtesy from* Fargo Forum*)*

The Stillwater County Jail, located behind the courthouse in Columbus, where the Downards were held after being falsely accused of the murders. *(Hattenburg photo)*

Chapter Four

The Confession

Sheriff Murphy felt that all of the pieces of the puzzle were falling into place. Larry's simple and direct statement that Frank Robideau had killed his parents was no surprise to him. Murphy felt satisfaction that he was one step closer to fully solving this case. He was tired but seeing the battered boy, and hearing absolute fear in his voice, gave new energy to the kind, gentle sheriff.

Murphy thanked Larry and reassured him that everything would be all right. He then left the boy resting and sought out Dr. Smith. He wanted to collect the piece of wood that had been embedded in the boy's skull. The doctor had been very careful in collecting that evidence. He had wrapped it in a piece of clean cloth to preserve it. He told the sheriff that he had not cleaned or touched it any more than needed.

As Murphy strode rapidly down the hospital corridor to return to his office, the evidence he and the other officers had been compiling ran through his mind. So far they knew of the large check that had been written out to Robideau and his false identification of the hitchhikers as the possible murderers. Frank was also the only person the officers interviewed who did not have a solid alibi for his whereabouts the night the killings took place. Murphy was certain that Robideau had tried to intimidate Larry at the general store as well as in his hospital room. Upon questioning individuals about the horrible incident, officers found that Frank was a close neighbor of Mike Kuntz. He would have known that Mike often parked his car in the elevator and would walk the short distance home from work. Living in such close proximity, Frank would have seen Mike drive home the night of the killings. He could have seen or heard the Kuntz family leave in their car and head out toward Columbus, flagging them down on their way.

Of course, the most compelling piece of evidence was the eyewitness identification of Robideau by the little boy. Larry was now more coherent. Murphy was certain from the tone and body language of the boy that Larry had told him the simple truth when he had accused Frank.

When Murphy arrived back at the jail, Benjamin greeted him with incredible news. He had received a phone call from Herschel Slavens while Murphy was at the hospital with Larry. Slavens was the owner of Slavens Lumber and Mercantile in the town of Molt, a very small town located about eight miles from Wheat Basin. Slavens was also the United States post master in Molt. He told Benjamin that on Saturday, a gentleman named Fred Sheets, who hauled freight from Billings to the local towns of Rapelje, Wheat Basin, and Molt, came in. When Sheets entered the store, there was a man with him that Slavens recognized as Frank Robideau. It turned out Robideau had come to the store in order to cash a couple of checks.

Slavens briefly looked at the checks and handed over the cash to Robideau. After that, Robideau quickly left the store saying that he had important business to take care of. Fred Sheets told Slavens and the other customers that were in the store about the terrible murders that had taken place the previous evening in Wheat Basin. They were all in shock at the news of the tragedy that had befallen the friendly and well-liked Kuntz family. Mr. Sheets said that officers at the scene had found some check stubs, and he shared the information about the register found in the elevator office of Mike Kuntz. Evidently, during his deliveries, Sheets had heard from some other locals that there were new potential leads in the case. As he was leaving the store on his way to Billings, Sheets again expressed his dismay and shock over the tragic news. He and the others hoped that a suspect would be apprehended soon.

Sheets' information caused Slavens to wonder about the checks he had just cashed. Slavens explained to Benjamin that when he cashed Robideau's two checks he did not examine them closely. There was no reason to be suspicious of them. Slavens had dealt with Robideau many times before. He often peddled vegetables and needed small checks cashed quite regularly. Later, when Slavens examined the checks more thoroughly, he discovered one was made out by Mike Kuntz, of the Wheat Basin Occident Grain Elevator, to a woman he had never heard of. This set off alarm bells in Slavens's mind.

Robideau had a peculiar way of endorsing checks by writing his name lengthwise on the back instead of across the end as was customary. On this particular check, both his name and that of the other person had been written lengthwise. When Slavens told the other fellows in the store about it, they advised him not to get involved as a murderer was still on the loose. After thinking about it all night, and considering the possible ramifications that the check could have as potential evidence, Slavens felt that it was important to contact the sheriff's office.

Sheriff Murphy quickly grabbed the phone and contacted Herschel Slavens at his store in Molt. He thanked him for this valuable information and asked him to come to the courthouse in Columbus later that evening with the check.

Murphy made a decision: it was time for him to act. When Murphy got off the phone with Mr. Slavens, he turned to Benjamin and shared with him the conversation that he had with the little Kuntz boy. The undersheriff reacted with great excitement. With the eyewitness identification, and the rest of the evidence, they could now arrest Frank Robideau and bring him in. Murphy and Benjamin were anxious to put the wheels of justice into motion. The sheriff put in a call to County Attorney Pat Heily. He let him know that, with all the recent developments in the case, they were now ready to go to Wheat Basin and place Frank Robideau under arrest for murder. The officers expected to return to the courthouse in a couple of hours and would meet him there.

Murphy and Benjamin, accompanied by Constables Earl Wilson and Albert Thomas of Billings, hurriedly climbed in to the sheriff's car and drove to Wheat Basin as quickly as the roads would allow. Murphy and Benjamin felt it was incredible that they were on the cusp of concluding this case in such a relatively short period of time. They also discussed with Thomas and Wilson the strategies they would use for the intense interrogation they planned in order to elicit a confession from Frank. All of the officers agreed that this would not be an easy task given Robideau's erratic behavior throughout the investigation.

As the men approached the small home of Frank Robideau at about 11 a.m., they saw him standing on the front porch smoking a cigarette. Frank greeted them in a surly manner and asked if the officers were in need of his help again. Murphy replied that it would not be necessary, as they were there to arrest him for the murders of the Kuntz couple.

As Benjamin handcuffed him, Robideau loudly argued his innocence. The lawmen were unmoved and put Frank in the back seat of the sheriff's car. Murphy seated himself beside Robideau in the back seat. Hearing the commotion outside, May quickly ran out to see what was going on. Constable Wilson explained to her that they were taking Frank in for questioning regarding the Kuntz killings and would be in contact with her later on that afternoon or evening. May began frantically yelling out to Frank to explain what the constable was talking about. The sheriff's car sped away, leaving her questions unanswered.

On the trip back to the jail and courthouse in Columbus, the officers gathered their energy for the final push to get Robideau to confess. A quick and just solution to the case would make all the long, hard hours and little sleep worthwhile. Murphy was looking forward to a quiet meal with his wife.

When they arrived at the courthouse, Pat Heily and Deputy Albert Jansen of Yellowstone County met them. Murphy was told Deputy Jansen was going to a back room of the courthouse to analyze and organize the physical evidence that had been collected. The first order of business was to have Robideau write on a piece of paper "We are closed today." With his hand visibly shaking, he complied and wrote out the words that had been found on the sign. Deputy Jansen immediately started a comparison of his handwriting to that of the note found on the door of the Occident Grain Elevator.

The other officers began the long, grueling process of questioning Robideau. Heily and the team grilled Robideau relentlessly for eight long hours. He was aggressively protesting his innocence, but the men countered every denial of his guilt. They exposed his lies with the evidence on hand, especially confronting him with the statement little Larry had made to Sheriff Murphy.

While the interrogation was underway, Herschel Slavens arrived at the courthouse, accompanied by the Molt Occident Elevator manager. Sheriff Murphy greeted them, and they went to a separate room where Slavins gave Murphy the check he had cashed for Robideau. Murphy noted Robideau's signature written laterally across the back of it. The sheriff asked the men from Molt to wait until the officers could confront Robideau with this new evidence. He then took the check back to Deputy Jansen for handwriting analysis.

While Mr. Slavens was waiting, he saw May Robideau, along with her children, in an outer office, nervously pacing around the room. May had come to find out what the charges were against her husband. No one had yet contacted her about the ongoing situation. She asked anyone available where he was and what was going on. May was getting increasingly worried. She had no income, no money for food, and she was pregnant. All May learned was that they were still questioning her husband and would get word to her soon. To Slavens it was evident that the officers felt her husband was close to breaking down and kept the pressure on him.

Murphy came back into the room and asked Slavens to verify the statements he had made to him over the phone earlier that day. Mr. Slavens again shared with the sheriff the appearance of Robideau at his store the day before, stating he quickly went on his way after the checks were cashed.

Mr. Slavens also reiterated to Murphy that he had cashed checks for Robideau the last few months when he was selling vegetables in the area. Slavens recalled one particular time when he was complaining about his lack of funds. Slavens had asked him why he didn't go to Columbus and sign up for relief in order to get some assistance for his family. Slavens explained to him that he and May would be able to qualify for financial assistance from the government. All he would have to do is fill out some paperwork and get fingerprinted.

Robideau nervously asked Slavens why they would need fingerprints if he were going to sign the paperwork anyway. Slavens replied that in order to prevent duplication of names and attempted fraud, the fingerprints would enable officials to positively identify an individual. Slavens stressed to him that during these hard economic times there were millions of people in the same situation. It was nothing to be ashamed of. Slavens was puzzled at Robideau's adamant refusal to be fingerprinted. He said that he didn't want the government interfering in his personal life and would not subject himself to their scrutiny.

Murphy sensed that this information about Robideau was important, but he was not sure how it fit in. Yet he was grateful to Slavens. The trip from Molt was not an easy one it was good of him to make the drive to Columbus. It was decent people like this that made Murphy determined to do his very best. With a sigh, Murphy put on his sternest game face and rejoined the interrogation.

Undersheriff Benjamin took Robideau's fingerprints and informed him they had an expert who was analyzing the prints found on the car. He would be comparing them to his prints. Benjamin also told him the officer was a handwriting expert as well and was comparing his handwriting to the writing on the sign from the elevator door. Watching for Robideau's reaction, Benjamin told him these items, as well as a check that he cashed in Molt at the store owned by Herschel Slavens, were being sent to the FBI crime lab for further analysis. This made him start to sweat.

Robideau continued to maintain his innocence until around 10:30 p.m. that Sunday evening. Finally, the eight grueling hours of relentless questioning and mounting evidence against him wore him down. There was no way any of his plans would work now. Every one of his efforts to point the blame elsewhere was exposed. With his attempted deceptions lying in tatters, he knew he was caught. He suddenly blurted out, "I did it. I killed him. He was yellow."

Robideau's confession was in the presence of Sheriff Murphy, Undersheriff Benjamin, and Constables Albert Thomas and Earl Wilson. It was at the threshold of this statement that the sheriff likely began to realize who the coward was. It was Robideau, the man who had just shot and killed two people, ambush style, in front of their five-year-old-son, and then beat the boy, in an attempt to kill him.

About twenty minutes later, Pat Heily presented Robideau with a fully written statement of his admission to the killings of Mike and Frieda Kuntz. Signing the document he gave up trying to hide his guilt, but that was only the beginning of his lies in attempts to justify his actions. He commenced to tell everyone present there were many circumstances the investigation team was not aware of. Again, the sheriff's thoughts must have turned to how pathetic, thoughtless, and self-serving this man's lies were.

Robideau was determined to spin his tale of what happened, perhaps to escape hanging, perhaps to ease his own conscience. Over the course of the next few hours, he tried one story after another. Murphy noted his many inaccuracies, carefully recording each one. Robideau would continue to repeat his half-truths and lies throughout his court appearances and his time in jail.

In his confession, he stated, "I had a quarrel with Kuntz because he would not pay me for my share of 180 bushels of wheat, stating that there were liens against it. I told him he could give me a check in the name of another farmer, and I would cash it. Kuntz then drew a gun on me, and I said, 'OK, we'll shoot it out.'

"He later came to my place with his wife and kid in the car and I climbed in the back seat." 'Drive to where you want to die,' I told him. 'He drove toward Columbus and suddenly stopped the car.' "Go ahead and shoot me, he said. I shot him through the back of the head and then shot Mrs. Kuntz through the breast. The kid started fighting, so I hit him with the gun handle and drove the car back to the elevator where I left it."

Investigators believed a version much closer to what had actually happened. They didn't know of Robideau's appearance at the Kuntz home that evening. Therefore, to place the family in the car, they concluded that Mike Kuntz was headed for Columbus that evening so he could report to the sheriff. It seemed logical that Mike would take his family with him for safety as he went to report that Robideau had forced him to write checks at gunpoint that afternoon in his office at the grain elevator.

To the investigating team's reasoning, Robideau had seen Mike Kuntz and his family get into their car from his home nearby and was afraid they were on their way to Columbus. He feared what Mike would say when he made his report to the police. The investigators figured he ran to the main street and flagged down the car. As Mike pulled over, he held the family at gunpoint and got in the back seat, ordering Mike to continue driving. The sheriff's version of what had happened was close, but not exactly what had occurred.

In their view, Mike had to have been visibly shaken and understandably nervous. After he drove about 12 miles out of town, Robideau demanded that he pull over to the side of the road. This was where it looked as though the car had stopped, at least momentarily. It then pulled back on to the road and proceeded about another half mile farther south. This was where the officers found the shattered glass and blood. He shot Mike first, and then tried to shoot Frieda but there had been a struggle. During the struggle, the remaining shots were fired and the last one killed Frieda. He then turned to the little boy. Perhaps he was angry that he was now out of ammunition. Consequently, he brutally beat Larry until he was unconscious, leaving him for dead. The sheriff was sure that if he had known that Larry was still alive, he would have finished what he intended to do. Knowing that Mike would often park it in the grain elevator, he then drove the car back toward Wheat Basin.

After placing the car inside the elevator, with what he thought were three lifeless bodies inside, Robideau closed the large door and attached the sign that he had hoped would divert any attention away from himself. To further lead investigators astray, he planned to implicate the hitchhikers at the town store the next morning.

The officers did not believe Robideau's account of the events, trying to paint Mike Kuntz as an instigator of violence. The evidence that they had collected pointed at him as the sole aggressor. Even if he had been owed for 180 bushels of wheat as he claimed, the price of wheat was 96 cents per bushel that fall, resulting in a total of approximately $170, not the excessive amount of the $675 check that he had forced Mike to write. To the lawmen, this meant greed and desperation were motives for the murders.

Sheriff Murphy and Undersheriff Benjamin felt sure that, with his wife and child in the car, there was no way Mike Kuntz would stop and voluntarily give Robideau a ride when he knew he had a gun. Mike knew he was armed and dangerous, because he had already threatened his life that day at the elevator.

Robideau's other story was even more unlikely. It was just too out of character for Mike Kuntz to have tried to accost him with his family present. From talking with people in the area, it was known that Mike Kuntz did not own a gun. He would not have threatened Robideau, nor would he put himself in a position to fight a duel. Robideau was lying again. His claims that he and Mike were going to have a shoot-out that night would have been virtually impossible. It was completely dark and there was not a light of any kind near or at the location where the murders took place. There was no shoot-out, of that they were certain.

The officers did not have Larry's entire eyewitness version of the events of Friday night, as he was still in the hospital recovering from his head wounds and a severe concussion. Larry was the only one who knew that Robideau had been in the Kuntz home on the night of the murders.

Soon after Robideau signed his confession, Undersheriff Benjamin made a press release. About 11 p.m. Sunday evening, the sheriff's office announced to waiting reporters about Robideau's admission of the mur-

The .38 caliber Smith and Wesson that Frank Robideau used in the murders of the Kuntzes is on display at the Museum of the Beartooths in Columbus, Montana. Penny Redli is the museum's curator. *(Hattenburg photo)*

ders of the popular young couple. The news traveled like wildfire throughout the small communities, and most of the residents knew of the confession, even before the Monday morning papers carried the story.

The outrage of the community was so intense that the officers were concerned for Robideau's safety. Benjamin had already received a call from an unidentified person in Molt warning him that there was a rising tide of anger towards Robideau. The lawmen all felt it would be better to place him in the Yellowstone County Jail in Billings, 36 miles away, for "safe keeping." The jail had a high-security, solitary-confinement cell, as opposed to the more open jail in Columbus.

Prior to having Officers Thomas and Wilson take him to Billings, Sheriff Murphy paid a visit to May Robideau. He told her she could speak to her husband briefly. Murphy felt sorry for the young woman. She and her children had nothing but desperately hard times ahead of them. With what Murphy had come to expect from his typical arrogant manner, Robideau told her not to worry and assured her he would take care of everything. Watching the officers lead her husband away in handcuffs, May was numb with shock at the circumstances she was now confronted with. May was expecting another child any day. She and the children were struggling to get by as it was. Now her husband was in jail, and she had to face the humiliation of telling her family and children what had happened. Apparently her own husband had murdered her best option for a midwife in Wheat Basin.

While Robideau was being transported to Billings, Murphy had another exhausting round trip to Wheat Basin to make that night. During his confession, Robideau had told Sheriff Murphy that he had buried the gun used in the shooting deaths of Mike and Frieda Kuntz in his back yard. The sheriff needed to retrieve the gun. It was about midnight Sunday when Murphy found where the soil had been recently dug up in Robideau's yard. He soon unearthed the gun, along with a box of cartridges, from the hole that was just a few feet west of the Robideau home. The weapon was a .38 caliber Smith and Wesson pistol. He also found a set of blackened, charred keys in the same hiding place. When he returned to his office, Murphy carefully examined the pistol and noticed the handle had dried blood on it and a small piece of wood was missing. When he compared the piece of wood that had been given to him by Dr. Smith to the hard lacquered handle of the gun belonging to Robideau, it was a perfect match. Murphy had hardly slept Saturday night, but now he was finally able to go home, knowing that the killer was in custody and the community was safe once again.

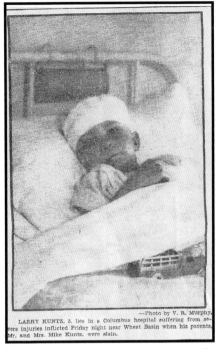

—Photo by V. R. Murphy.
LARRY KUNTZ, 5, lies in a Columbus hospital suffering from severe injuries inflicted Friday night near Wheat Basin when his parents, Mr. and Mrs. Mike Kuntz, were slain.

Early Monday morning November 29, after getting a few hours of much needed sleep, Murphy went to the hospital to check on Larry's condition. He met up with the little boy's Aunt Genevieve and Uncle Val. They had arrived on the train that morning and had gone straight to the hospital. Murphy liked the two relatives right away. They were very concerned for Larry and, despite their grief over losing Mike and Frieda, it seemed likely they would take very good care of the little boy.

Monday morning the 29th of November, Aunt Genevieve arrived to stay with Larry while he recovered in the hospital. Notice the little fire truck on the bed. Larry received gifts from all over the United States as the story of his near death and the murders of his parents became news. *(Photo by Victor Murphy, courtesy* the *Billings Gazette)*

Murphy related the good news of Robideau's arrest and confession, assuring them the killer was safely locked away in a cell in Billings. Genevieve and Val were ecstatic with the news. Val cast a long look at Larry resting in his bed near them, then turned and asked Murphy a set of very important questions: "Will Larry need to be questioned any further by you or any other officers? Will he need to appear at the trial to identify the killer?"

Murphy replied that, even though the boy was quickly improving, he was concerned for his emotional state. All three of them agreed that if Robideau could be convicted without Larry's testimony, it would avoid the agony of the child being placed on the witness stand and having to relive that horrible night. Because of this conversation, the officers did not pursue any further questioning of the small boy.

With Larry's aunt now staying with him at the hospital, Murphy felt relieved. Knowing Larry was with a loving family member and his condition was continually improving took a big worry off his mind.

When Murphy returned to his office, Benjamin let him know he had received a phone call from federal authorities that the Downard's fingerprints had cleared them of any previous criminal activity. The officers had expected as much. Sheriff Murphy released them and insisted on giving them a ride back to their small shack. It was a cold, wintry day, and he felt it was the right thing to do.

The trail of terror that Robideau had created by accusing them of cold-blooded murder continued to plague the Downards. When they arrived at the shack where they were staying, they found that someone in the outraged community had entered their cabin, taken their few articles of clothing outside and burned them. Worse yet, their shaggy little black dog had been run over and killed by a vehicle during the rampage.

Fortunately, their rickety automobile had been left undamaged by the vigilantes during the destruction of their belongings. A dusting of new snow covered any evidence the sheriff could have used to find out who had done this to the innocent couple and their pet.

The Downards were devastated by the loss of their dog. They had gone from relief at finding a warm ride to Columbus, to the anxiety of being murder suspects, to thankfulness at Murphy's generosity, and now to grief, all in a few days.

Sheriff Murphy was grim. His foresight in protecting the Downards may have proven fortunate, but he was unhappy about the circumstances that followed Robideau's accusation. By that afternoon, with the approval of the county commissioners, the sheriff was able procure money as well as gas for their antiquated automobile, to help them leave town. The Downards left the area on December 1, saying that they were going to the state of Washington to look for work. They understood the outrage of the community over the murder of such fine people. They didn't understand how Robideau could be so cold and evil.

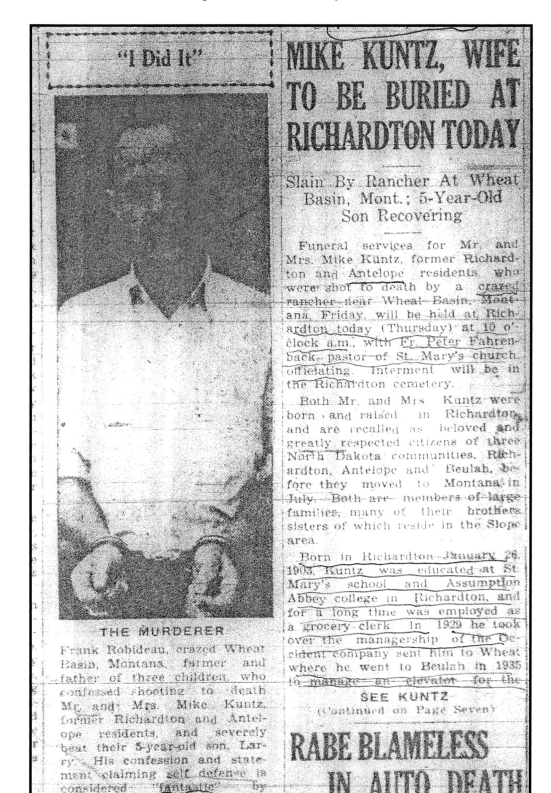

"I Did It"

THE MURDERER

Frank Robideau, crazed Wheat Basin, Montana, farmer and father of three children, who confessed shooting to death Mr. and Mrs. Mike Kuntz, former Richardton and Antelope residents, and severely beat their 5-year-old son, Larry. His confession and statement claiming self defense is considered "fantastic" by

MIKE KUNTZ, WIFE TO BE BURIED AT RICHARDTON TODAY

Slain By Rancher At Wheat Basin, Mont.; 5-Year-Old Son Recovering

Funeral services for Mr. and Mrs. Mike Kuntz, former Richardton and Antelope residents who were shot to death by a crazed rancher near Wheat Basin, Montana, Friday, will be held at Richardton today (Thursday) at 10 o'clock a.m., with Fr. Peter Fahrenback, pastor of St. Mary's church officiating. Interment will be in the Richardton cemetery.

Both Mr. and Mrs. Kuntz were born and raised in Richardton, and are recalled as beloved and greatly respected citizens of three North Dakota communities, Richardton, Antelope and Beulah, before they moved to Montana in July. Both are members of large families, many of their brothers sisters of which reside in the Slope area.

Born in Richardton January 26, 1903, Kuntz was educated at St. Mary's school and Assumption Abbey college in Richardton, and for a long time was employed as a grocery clerk. In 1929 he took over the managership of the Occident company sent him to Wheat where he went to Beulah in 1935 to manage an elevator for the

SEE KUNTZ
(Continued on Page Seven)

RABE BLAMELESS IN AUTO DEATH

News article following Frank Robideau's confession. *(Dickinson Press)*

Chapter Five
The Coroner's Inquest

On Monday afternoon, November 29, a coroner's inquest was held in Columbus. County Attorney Pat R. Heily introduced an unearthed revolver and a handwritten sign as evidence supporting the confession of Robideau. Robideau admitted that he slew his neighbors, Mike and Frieda Kuntz.

The following is the transcribed testimony (in its entirety and exactly as it was written) from the coroner's inquest regarding the deaths of Mike and Frieda Kuntz:

> Subscribed and sworn to before me this 29th day of November 1937 BEFORE THE CORONER OF STILLWATER COUNTY, MONTANA IN THE MATTER OF THE INQUEST HELD ON THE BODIES OF MIKE KUNTZ AND FRIEDA KUNTZ, Deceased
>
> TESTIMONY OF WITNESSES
>
> BE IT REMEMBERED, that at the courtroom of the court house in the City of Columbus, Stillwater County, Montana, before O. R. McColley, coroner of said county and state, at the hour of three o'clock p.m. November 29, 1937, was held the inquest on the bodies of Mike Kuntz and Frieda Kuntz, then lying dead in the funeral parlors of McColley's Furniture Store [the funeral parlor and furniture store were in the same building]; that at said time and place witnesses were called, sworn by the coroner of Stillwater County, Montana, and examined by P. R. Heily, Esquire, County Attorney of said county.
>
> G. B. Iverson appeared at the request of said Coroner to take the testimony of the witnesses directly upon the typewriter and the same was duly sworn to correctly take down and transcribe the proceedings so had.
>
> And the jurors, having duly been sworn and having viewed the bodies of the deceased Mike Kuntz and Frieda Kuntz, the following proceedings were had:

O. R. Ray McColley was the county coroner and also the owner of the furniture store in Columbus. McColley performed the autopsies on Mike and Frieda and was in charge of the coroner's inquest. *(Courtesy Museum of the Beartooths)*

J. S. Benjamin, called as a witness in said inquisition, being first duly sworn, upon examination by Mr. Heily, testified as follows:

Q. Will you state your name and business?

A. J. S. Benjamin, Undersheriff of Stillwater County, Montana.

Q. How many years have you lived in this community?

A. I have lived in Columbus about 10 or 12 years.

Q. You were called to investigate an alleged shooting out in the Basin country Saturday morning, November 27th, 1937?

A. Yes.

Q. And when you went out there what did you find?

A. I found the bodies of Mike Kuntz and his wife, Frieda Kuntz, dead in a car in the elevator at Wheat Basin, Montana.

Q. Could you tell the apparent cause of their death?

A. They had been shot, and apparently murdered.

Q. Did you arrest anyone in connection with the alleged crime?

A. Yes. We arrested Frank Robideau.

Q. You were present when he confessed?

A. Yes.

Q. You saw him sign the confession after it was written out?

A. Yes.

Q. That is all.

McColley's furniture store in Columbus, in the 1930s. *(Alice McColley collection, courtesy Museum of the Beartooths)*

McColley's Funeral Home, located in the back of the furniture store. *(Alice McColley collection, courtesy Museum of the Beartooths)*

FRANK MURPHY, called as a witness in said inquisition, being first duly sworn, upon examination by P. R. Heily, testified as follows:

Q. Will you state your name and business?

A. Frank Murphy, Sheriff of Stillwater County, Montana.

Q. How many years have you lived in this community?

A. I have lived at Columbus about 7 years.

Q. You have heard the testimony relative to the alleged crime committed in Stillwater County, Montana on or about November 27th, 1937?

A. Yes.

Q. Upon investigation what did you find?

A. The bodies of Mike Kuntz and Frieda Kuntz at the elevator at Wheat Basin, Montana.

Q. Did you ascertain the cause of death?

A. They had been shot several times each.

Q. And was there anyone arrested in connection therewith?

A. Yes, we arrested Frank Robideau.

Q. And you questioned him about the matter?

A. Yes, he finally confessed.

Q. He finally confessed in your presence did he?

A. Yes, he confessed he shot both, that he shot Kuntz and his wife and struck the boy with the gun.

Q. That is all.

WILLIAM P. SMITH, called as a witness in said inquisition, being first duly sworn, upon examination by Mr. Heily, testified as follows:

Q. Will you state your name and business?

A. William P. Smith, physician and surgeon.

Q. And you reside at Columbus, Montana?

A. Yes, sir.

Q. And how long have you been in practice at Columbus?

A. 25 years.

Q. And you are a duly licensed physician and surgeon of the State?

A. Yes, sir.

Q. And did you wait upon the bodies of Mike Kuntz and Frieda Kuntz, his wife?

A. Yes, sir.

Q. And will you tell us what you found?

A. I examined the bodies.

Q. Can you state to the jury the cause of their death?

A. The man came to his death as a result of a gunshot wound. The bullet entered the body at a point two inches behind and one-half inch below the lobe of the right ear, traversed the neck in an upward and forward direction with point of exit at the tip of the lobe of the left ear. The bullet shattered the spinal column and severed the cord just below the base of the skull.

The woman came to her death as the result of a gunshot wound. The bullet entered the body at a point one and one-half inch above the nipple line and one-half inch to the right of the midline. It pursued a course downward and to the left and its point of exit was one inch below the angle of the left scapula at about three inches to the left of the mid line of the back. The bullet passed through the heart.

Q. That is all.

Judge. If there is anyone in this audience here present, that has anything to give in the way of testimony to clear up this inquisition at this time, now is the chance to do so. If you have any information to give, anybody present, please come forward.

No Response.

The following is the coroner's verdict as reported in the *Columbus News*, December 2, 1937:

CORONER'S VERDICT

STATE OF MONTANA
County of Stillwater

An Inquisition, held at the courtroom of the courthouse in Columbus in the County of Stillwater, State of Montana, on the 29th of November, A.D. 1937, before me, O. R. McCollay, coroner of said County of Stillwater, upon the bodies of Mike Kuntz and Frieda Kuntz, there lying dead, by the jurors, whose names are hereunto subscribed. The said jurors upon their oaths do say, that from the evidence provided them said Mike Kuntz and Frieda Kuntz came to their death from gunshot wounds, inflicted by one Frank Robideau.

The names of the six jurors followed. They were: W. E. Boston, Roy Jones, R. L. Duba, W. H. Hillstead, P. F. Morrison, and P. E. Hagland. [The newspaper account continued with additional information about the case, some of which is summarized in the subsequent text.]

Following the coroner's inquest, the bodies of Mr. and Mrs. Kuntz were taken by a Northern Pacific train to the home of their births in Richardton, North Dakota. They were accompanied by Mike Kuntz's brother, Valentine S. Kuntz, and left Columbus at 11:30 that evening of November 29, 1937. Both Mike and Frieda had numerous siblings and relatives in the area and funeral arrangements were still pending.

County Attorney Heily announced to the press the results of the coroner's inquest, and that he had filed a complaint charging Frank Robideau with first degree murder in the deaths of Mike and Frieda Kuntz. He told reporters that public indignation was running high in the Wheat Basin country as a result of the slayings of the couple and the beating of their five-year-old son, Larry Kuntz.

Heily gave the details of the sign that had been posted on the grain elevator, and announced that handwriting expert Deputy Sheriff Albert Jansen of Yellowstone County said Robideau's handwriting was "identical" with that on the sign. Even though he had confessed to the murders of the Kuntz couple, Robideau continued to deny that he was the person who wrote and posted the sign. In a press interview with Robideau from the Yellowstone County Jail in Billings, he told a *Billings Gazette* reporter, "I'm going to plead not guilty by reason of self-defense."

On Tuesday, November 30, Undersheriff Jack Benjamin announced to the press gathered in Columbus: "Robideau's story is not logical." Benjamin added that officers are continuing this investigation in an effort to unearth the true facts in the dual slaying on the Wheat Basin-Columbus Road on Friday evening.

On one of their visits to the hospital, little Larry Kuntz, five-year-old survivor of the death ride, reiterated his story to Benjamin. According to the December 2, 1937, *Columbus News*, Larry told Benjamin, "We were driving toward Columbus and 'Bing' ["bing" was the term Larry used to describe the sound of the gun], Robideau shot Papa, then shot Mama and he hit me."

"I believe the little boy," Benjamin said.

Benjamin also said, "Robideau was in the Visser store at Wheat Basin when Larry walked in the morning after the slaying. I believe Robideau put the hitchhikers into Larry's mind and the youngster, somewhat dazed, believed the story for a short time. Mr. and Mrs. Kuntz were dressed in their work clothes, not their party clothes, as they were in a hurry, I believe, to get to Columbus and report the wheat deal."

The investigation revealed that Robideau forced Kuntz to write the wheat checks and Benjamin believed that Robideau threatened Kuntz with death if Kuntz revealed the check transactions. He surmised that Kuntz, his wife, and child were en route to Columbus to report Robideau to the sheriff's office when Robideau stopped the Kuntz automobile. "I believe he shot Kuntz when he failed to turn back to Wheat Basin. Kuntz had no gun so I believe the duel [story] is bunk."

Wednesday, December 1, with the investigation continuing, Benjamin said no new angles had been uncovered up to that afternoon, but they were attempting to obtain the true facts in one of the most tragic incidents in the history of the state of Montana.

While Frank awaited trial in the Yellowstone County Jail, two families mourned the loss of their son and daughter, sister and brother in Richardton, North Dakota. The double funeral for Mike and Frieda Kuntz was held on Thursday, December 2, at St. Mary's Catholic Church of Richardton. This was the same church that Mike and Frieda had been married in eight years earlier.

Over one thousand sorrowing friends and relatives crowded into the church to pay their respects. It was the largest gathering the church had ever seen. People came from many surrounding North Dakota communities. The Kuntzes' friends from Wheat Basin also made the journey to attend. The church was filled with countless floral arrangements expressing condolences to the two families. As Mike and Frieda were buried side by side in the St. Mary's Cemetery, little Larry was lying in a hospital bed in Columbus recuperating from his injuries.

The grave site of Mike and Frieda Kuntz, located in the St. Mary's Cemetery, Richardton, North Dakota. *(Photo from Findagrave.com)*

Chapter Six

First Court Appearance

After having been in a solitary confinement cell for four days, Frank readied himself for his first court appearance relating to the charges filed by County Attorney Heily in the deaths of Mike and Frieda Kuntz. For the first time since he entered the doors of the Yellowstone County Jail in Billings, he shaved his heavy growth of whiskers in the jail barbershop. While washing his face, Frank stared at the reflection in the mirror and must have been wondering how he could have allowed his temper to get the best of him. He was in serious trouble once again. Frank knew that May and their children must be suffering from the humiliation of his dastardly deeds and the shame of his arrest. Jailer E. J. Oldridge, who had been closely guarding him, interrupted Frank's thoughts. Oldridge told Frank that Sheriff Stephenson was due to arrive momentarily and transport him to the courthouse in Columbus.

Accompanied by Constables Wilson and Thomas, the sheriff and his officers handcuffed Robideau and shackled him at the ankles. They led him outside to a vehicle parked alongside the curb in front of the jail. With the constables on either side of him, Frank probably glanced around the downtown area and wondered if he would ever be free to walk the streets again. Lost in thought, Frank was in a somber mood. It made the ride to Columbus an exceptionally quiet journey.

The crowd in Columbus was a sharp contrast to the empty countryside they had just traveled through. People were gathered, not only inside the courthouse and hallways but also on the grounds outside. Friends of the Kuntz family and curious onlookers, anticipating the arrival of Frank, filled every available spot. Immediately after reaching their destination, the small contingent exited the vehicle. For many people in attendance that day, it was the first time they had ever seen Frank without a beard.

Sheriff Murphy and his officers met the group and surrounded Robideau as they made their way up the stairs into the Stillwater County Courthouse. Frank kept his head down, avoiding eye contact with anyone, and restrained himself from having any verbal exchanges with the subdued spectators.

On Friday afternoon, December 3, 1937, Robideau was brought before Judge Ben Harwood in front of a packed courtroom to face two counts of the charge of first-degree murder. County Attorney Pat Heily officially filed the charges. In a surprise move, Robideau changed his plea of not guilty to that of guilty of murder in the first degree of Mike Kuntz. However, he pled not guilty to a first-degree murder charge in connection with the slaying of Frieda Kuntz.

The Stillwater County Courthouse in Columbus, where Robideau was led up the stairs to face murder charges on December 3, 1937. *(Hattenburg photo)*

The bench from which Judge Ben Harwood presided over a packed courtroom of curious spectators on December 3, 1937.
(Hattenburg photo)

Attorneys for the defense were E. A. Blenkner and M. L. Parcells. They were paid $100 for defending Frank Robideau in the case. The following is a transcript of the appearance held at the Stillwater County Courthouse as printed in the *Columbus News* December 9, 1937:

The Court: The court will come to order. Mr. County Attorney, have you any matter that you wish to present to the court?

Mr. Heily: At this time, if the court please, I wish to file on behalf of the State, a motion for the leave to file an information in the case of the State of Montana vs. Frank Robideau.

The Court: Let the record show that the motion of the county attorney is granted.

Mr. Heily: At this time I offer for filing in this court an information on behalf of the State of Montana, charging Frank Robideau with the crime of the murder of one Frieda Kuntz. (As Frank had confessed to killing Mike Kuntz in cold blood and pled guilty to that charge, no motion was filed regarding that charge.) A motion was filed for Frieda's killing as Frank claimed he killed Frieda in self-defense.

Mr. Heily: I understand that the defendant is in court, your honor?

The Court: Very well, we will proceed with the arraignment. Is Frank Robideau in the courtroom? If so, let him stand. (The defendant stood before the bar of the court.)

The Court: Your true name is Frank Robideau?

The Defendant: Yes.

The Court: Are you represented by an attorney?

Mr. Robideau: No, I am not.

The Court: Have you any property or any other possessions so that you may employ an attorney?

Mr. Robideau: No, I have not.

The Court: The Court might say that in this type of case the court will not receive a plea from a defendant without his being represented by an attorney-at-law as counsel. I inform you, Mr. Defendant, that in this County of Stillwater we have three practicing attorneys, the County Attorney, Mr. Heily, and two others, M.L... Parcells and E. A. Blenkner. These attorneys are officers of the court and under the authority of the court.

Because of this situation the court now appoints to represent you in this case, The State of Montana vs. Frank Robideau, M.L. Parcells, Esq. and E.A. Blenkner, Esq., attorneys-at-law. I understand that Mr. Blenkner is not here and that Mr. Parcells is. Mr. Parcells, if there is not some good reason why you and Mr. Blenkner cannot accept the appointment to represent this man on the express order of this court, will you step forward and carry on this arraignment?

Mr. Parcells: I have no reason why, under the direction of the court, I cannot represent the defendant.

The Court: Very well, my duty is to inform the defendant that he may have time to consider the plea which he will make to the information as filed in this case, or the time may be waived and he may plead at this time. If you should care for a moment or two in which to consult with the defendant with reference to the waiving of time, you may have it.

Mr. Parcells: Very well your honor, the information may now be read.

(The clerk handed a document to the defendant.)

The Court: Yes the clerk may now read the information. I merely wanted the defendant to know about that incidentally, so that he would not speak before the information was read as so many times is done. In other words, so that he may have time for thought after the reading of this information. Mr. Clerk will you read the information on file? (Clerk read the information on file.)

Mr. Parcells: I should like, if your honor please, a few minutes in which to confer with the defendant.

The Court: You may possibly clear up some things if you consult with this defendant in here in this adjoining room. (Mr. Parcells and the defendant, accompanied by Sheriff Murphy, withdrew to an anteroom.)

Mr. Heily: If the court please, I notice that I have inadvertently inserted the 5th of December in the information instead of the 3rd. Will the court make the proper correction?

The Court: Let the record show that the Court has corrected the information to read the 3rd of December instead of the 5th of December.

(Mr. Parcells and the defendant, accompanied by the sheriff, return to the courtroom.)

Mr. Parcells: If the court pleases, the defendant will waive time in which to plead to the information and enter a plea at this time.

The Court: Let the record show that the defendant in open court, with counsel appointed by the court, now waives time in which to consider his plea and enter his plea at this time. Mr. Robideau, the court now asks you, what is your plea to the information in this case?

The Defendant: Not guilty (to the murder of Frieda Kuntz)

The Court: Let the record show that the defendant Frank Robideau enters a plea of not guilty to the information as charged. The defendant will appear in court on December 11, 1937, for a pre-trial hearing. The defendant will be remanded to the custody of the Sheriff of Stillwater County and remain jailed there until his next court appearance.

The Court is adjourned.

Four days later the newspaper reported that Tuesday night, December 7th, experts from the U.S. Department of Justice had informed Deputy Sheriff Albert Jansen by telegraph that the handwriting on the crude sign left on the door of the Wheat Basin elevator was indeed that of Frank Robideau. The sign, as well a check with his signature, and a sample of his handwriting, which he furnished officers following his arrest, had been sent to experts in Washington, D.C., for comparison.

But there was a shock waiting for everyone. Sheriff Murphy received a report from the U.S. Department of Justice stating that the fingerprints of Robideau were found on file at the Auburn Prison in New York State. However, the report stated the fingerprints were those of Joseph Liberty, convicted December 22, 1910, on a charge of murder in the second degree. Joseph Liberty had been sentenced from 20 years to life on that charge. He escaped from a prison road camp on July 25, 1922, and subsequently changed his identity. Robideau/Liberty had killed before!

When first confronted with this information, Robideau denied any involvement in this previous crime, and that he had never been known as Joseph Liberty. When the officers challenged him with the indisputable evidence of fingerprints from the F.B.I., he suddenly asked to have Mrs. Robideau brought to the jail to consult with her.

In the presence of Sheriff Murphy and Undersheriff Benjamin, Robideau/Liberty talked with Mrs. Robideau. "I got into another jam like this back in New York," Robideau told May.

This was the first indication that she had ever heard of this previous crime. Frank explained to her and the officers present that he had been sentenced to serve 20 years to life in Dannemora (correctly known as Clinton Prison) following his confession of guilt in Plattsburgh, New York. Ten years later, he was transferred to Auburn Prison where he was made a trustee. For time served, he was made a cook on a prison road crew. Camp jealousies resulted in an order that sent him back to Auburn Prison. Regulations inside Auburn were much more rigid and the daily routine harder to tolerate. Not wanting to endure the much tougher conditions inside the wall, he escaped.

After being on the lam for a while, Frank headed to New York City. He felt he could get lost in the heavily populated area of Manhattan. While there, he worked in various jobs including as a longshoreman and cook. Later, he headed to the city of Pittsburg, where he was employed at a box factory. Frank said that things began to look "pretty shaky" so he went further west for a time. He returned to New York City, but became frightened he would be caught and sent back to prison if he met acquaintances who knew of his escape. This time, Frank fled to Wyoming and, for a while was employed in the oil fields there. Later he came to the Wheat Basin country, where he was employed at the Downer farms.

Officers pointed out a discrepancy in Robideau's story. They noted that when arrested in Wheat Basin, he gave his age as 36. If that were true, he would have been 11 years old when sentenced in New York. If he had been that age, he would have served time in a reformatory rather than a prison. Given the fact that he was sentenced to prison in 1910 at the age of 21, Murphy and Benjamin believed Robideau to be 47-48 years old. Knowing Robideau's propensity for repeated lies and exaggerations, the officers decided not to question him about the circumstances regarding the murders in New York until they received more information from authorities in that state.

May Robideau was appalled beyond belief to know her entire married life with Frank had been a lie. When she met him about 1930, he had told her he was born in Wyoming. He lied about his name, age, and birthplace. Not only was he presently being tried for murder, he was also an escaped felon from New York for a double homicide committed 27 years ago. His name was not even Frank Robideau; it was Joseph Liberty. He was twelve years older than he told her when they met, making him 21 years older than she.

May not only was married to an escaped murderer, old enough to be her father, she had borne his children, and was expecting another at any time. This whole chain of events was unbelievable. May thought, "What else could possibly happen!"

After finding out that Robideau was an alias for Joseph Liberty, Murphy phoned the authorities in New York to let them know that they had Liberty in custody and that he would not be returning to their prison system. The Joseph Liberty/Frank Robideau arrest brought to a close a 15 year manhunt that had involved law enforcement officers throughout the United States.

ROBIDEAU FUGITIVE N.Y. MURDERER

Columbus, Mont.—Frank Robideau, Wheat Basin farmer, charged with the slaying of Mr. and Mrs. Mike Kuntz, former Richardton residents, is an escaped murderer from New York state, officials revealed Tuesday.

Robideau was convicted 20 years

This article in the *Dickinson Press* appeared shortly after Frank Robideau's fingerprints revealed he was an escaped murderer from prison in New York State. He and his brother had committed a thrill murder of a Civil War veteran and his brother.

Seated, from left to right: Prosecutor P. R. Heily; Sheriff Frank Murphy; and Undersheriff Jack Benjamin. *(Courtesy Victor Murphy)*

Chapter Seven

The Liberty Brothers

The people of the Plattsburgh, New York, area awoke to the following lead story in the *Plattsburgh Sentinel* on Monday morning, December 5, 1910:

> What may be the most dastardly and cold-blooded murder in the history of Northern New York has occurred in the town of Beekmantown. The murderers, little more than boys, confessed their crimes and are in jail awaiting a grand jury this week.
>
> On the evening of December 3, David and Newell Varno were shot by George Liberty, eighteen years of age, and Joseph Liberty twenty-one years of age. David Varno died at the scene, and his brother Newell is in critical condition at the Champlain Valley Hospital from multiple gun shot wounds.

Plattsburgh is on the western shores of Lake Champlain in the Hudson River Valley. This is a land of gently rolling hills, hardwood forests, and green grassy fields. The Saranac River runs through the city on its journey to Lake Champlain. Plattsburgh, thus known as "the Lake City," has a colorful history, starting with the native and French influence on it from early colonial times. These influences can still be felt in the present.

Approximately 62 miles south of Montreal, Canada, Plattsburgh began as the site of a French fur trading post as early as 1785. It was established as a village in 1815. The area around Plattsburgh had an abundance of timber for wood products. As more and more land was cleared for farming, it also became known for its fertile soil. The city itself was established in 1902.

The murders that shook the entire area took place at the log cabin home of David and Newell Varno. On the evening of December 3, about 9:30 p.m., Sheriff Robert Nash of Clinton County received a call from the home of Joseph Mouso, who informed him that a man had collapsed on his front porch. The man had apparently been shot. Mr. Mouso said that he had just retired for the evening and that, upon hearing a crashing sound on his front porch, threw a robe over his nightclothes and went out to investigate. He found his neighbor Newell Varno lying there in a pool of blood. After notifying Dr. Robert McDonald and Dr. John Robinson of Plattsburgh about the wounded man at the Mouso residence, as well as a possible murder scene at the Varno home, Sheriff Nash drove the six miles to the scene.

When he arrived at the small Varno home, Sheriff Nash found what he later described as a scene from a slaughterhouse. David, one of the Varno brothers, was lying in his bed. He had been shot in the head. The other brother, Newell, was covered with blood and in a semiconscious state at the Mouso home. Newell was still able to tell Sheriff Nash the murderers had identified themselves with the name Rivers, and they lived near Beartown, just north of there. He also gave a physical description of the two assailants. After tending to and temporarily dressing Newell Varno's wounds, Drs. McDonald and Robinson had him transported to the Champlain Valley Hospital.

Acting upon the information from Newell Varno, Sheriff Nash and Deputy Sheriff Stillwell started for Beartown, about ten miles farther north, in search of the Rivers brothers. At that time, there were many families by the name of Rivers who lived in that area, so it would not be an easy task for the officers to find their possible suspects. After a long night and morning interviewing various individuals, Sheriff Nash and Deputy Sheriff Stillwell took into custody two men by the last name of Rivers who fit the description of the shooters.

Coroner Henry L. Carpenter was at Varno's Champlain Valley Hospital bedside taking his antemortem statement when Newell Varno saw the two men brought in by the sheriff. He said right away that they were not the guilty parties. Sheriff Nash immediately released the Rivers men from custody and went back out to find the two individuals that were still at large. Because of the nature of the killings, he knew they were extremely dangerous.

Plattsburgh Police Chief Andrew Conners had spent most of the night at the gruesome murder scene with District Attorney Arthur Hogue. He had some remarkable success in securing evidence and information. The more he saw, the more convinced he became that the two Liberty brothers could have been involved in the shootings.

The Liberty brothers lived 12 miles north of Plattsburgh in the small town of West Chazy. One of the brothers, George Liberty, was at the home of his brother-in-law Fred Rivers, who lived at Beekmantown Corners.

Chief Conners set out to the Rivers' home and, upon arrival, found that George Liberty was indeed there. While he was talking to George, the chief noticed a pair of gloves lying on a table that looked to be duplicates of a pair found on the floor of the murder scene at the Varno home. He noted that the gloves were fairly small. The ones left behind at the scene were also small enough to fit someone of a younger age or stature. The canvas gloves were cut off at the wrist, just like the ones found at the murder scene.

In his conversation with Chief Conners, George Liberty told him that he and his brother Joseph had made an arrangement to secure a horse from a man named John Mullen. George explained that Joseph had ridden the horse to a church in West Chazy. Chief Conners then drove over to the Mullen house and was able to secure a crucial bit of evidence that could possibly connect the Liberty brothers to the earlier crime.

Eugene Richards worked for and lived with the Mullens. Eugene told Conners that, when arranging for the hiring of a horse the previous Saturday afternoon, one of the Liberty brothers asked him if he would be interested in going with them to hold up and rob travelers as they passed along the West Beekmantown Highway. Eugene asked the Liberty brothers how they would do this, and he was told that one of the brothers had a revolver. They would stop a rig as it came by and flash their gun in the driver's and passenger's faces. They would then order the victims to give up any money or valuables they might have. Richards told the chief that he refused to go along with this, and the Liberty brothers then left accompanied by a cousin named Frank Rivers.

By the time they had arrived at Halsey's Corners, Rivers also refused to go along with the hair-brained scheme of the Liberty brothers and went on his way. He continued to the home of an aunt in Plattsburgh, where he arrived about 8:30 p.m. He spent the rest of the night there. After this interview, Chief Conners returned to the home of Fred Rivers and took George Liberty into custody. He transported him to the sheriff's office in Plattsburgh, and placed him under arrest. Conners informed Sheriff Nash what he had learned. Acting on the chief's advice, Sheriff Nash and Deputy Stillwell quickly left in an attempt to apprehend Joseph Liberty.

After only a few hours, the sheriff and his deputy returned from West Chazy with Joseph Liberty in their custody. As they were driving back to the sheriff's office, the officers told Joseph Liberty that they had evidence from the scene of the crime that implicated him and his brother George. When informed by the officers that Newell Varno was still alive and would be able to identify the assailants, Joseph broke down weeping and suddenly to the amazement of the officers, made a complete confession. He stated that he had shot Newell Varno and his brother George had shot David Varno. In his confession, Joseph said that after the shootings, the brothers ran across some fields to their brother-in-law's house, throwing their revolvers in one of them along the way.

Once Joseph was locked in the cell with his brother George, the officers confronted George with the confession Joseph had presented to them on the drive back from West Chazy. For a time George vehemently denied his guilt, but Joseph was to have said, "What's the use denying it? We did it." George eventually broke down after Joseph's adamant statement and also admitted his part in the terrible crime.

They each refused the services of an attorney when offered to them. When asked of their motive, neither would admit it was robbery. They said they shot the old men for the fun of it. However, the officers believed a pension that Newell Varno received was the motive for the crime.

In a detailed confession, the brothers explained the order of the events that occurred on that cold winter night. The two brothers said they set out to rob travelers on the West Beekmantown Highway. They reached the home of David and Newell Varno around 8:30 p.m. on the night of December 3. After hearing a knock on the front door of his log cabin, the 65-year-old Newell encountered the Liberty brothers. The brothers asked if they could come in and get warm before continuing the walk to their home in Beekmantown. The brothers introduced themselves, giving their last name as Rivers.

Shortly before George's and Joseph's arrival, 58-year-old David Varno had retired for the evening and was asleep in an adjoining room. Newell let the two men enter the home and sat with them around a warm stove in the front room of the small dwelling. Engaging in light conversation, Newell had no idea the tragedy he and his brother would soon face.

After being in the house for about an hour, George Liberty said that it was about time that they moved on, as it was getting quite late. Joseph then told him to wait until he rolled a cigarette and put his hand in

It was not far from this location on the West Beekmantown Highway that the Liberty brothers arrived at the home of David and Newell Varno on December 3, 1910. *(Hattenburg photo)*

his pocket. Instead of removing tobacco and cigarette paper, he drew a revolver and fired at Newell Varno. The bullet entered Newell's right cheek near the nose and exited on the left side of his face near the jawbone. George Liberty rushed into David's room. He fired a shot that entered David's brain just over the right eye. Although he lived until the next morning, David Varno never stirred or regained consciousness.

Newell staggered to a nearby door and grabbed a shotgun that was propped up against the wall next to it. As he desperately attempted to defend himself, Joseph once again shot him. The bullet entered his left breast near the heart. Remarkably, the shot did not floor the man. Seeing that Newell was still standing, and that he had a shotgun, the Liberty brothers ran from the house into the dark wintry night.

Showing remarkable stamina, Newell stumbled out of his house and dragged himself across several fields. In incredible pain, the elderly man endured the cold winds that whipped around him as he struggled to the nearest home 150 yards away. He collapsed on the front porch of his landlord, Joseph Mouso. Mouso was horrified at Newell's condition and hurriedly called the police.

The morning following their arrest and confession, the Liberty brothers were handcuffed together and taken to the Champlain Valley Hospital, where Newell Varno was fighting for his life. There, Newell Varno positively identified them as the men who shot him and killed his brother David.

Joseph and George were the eighth and ninth children of John and Matilda (Rivers) Liberty. The family had been living near the town line between Plattsburgh and Beekmantown. Matilda had died in1899, leaving John to raise the six children that were still living at the home. By 1910, Joseph was working on the farm of William Loughan which was a short distance from the Liberty homestead. George, the youngest of the children, was still living at home and helping his father run the family farm.

The Libertys struggled to get by with what they could produce from the farm. Between the hard living and hard times, the youngest Liberty brothers were a bit wild. It was well known in the community that the two brothers often drank heavily on the weekends. They were always trying to find ways to get money to purchase the alcohol they consumed.

On December 13, just ten days after the shootings, indictments for first-degree murder against the Liberty brothers were filed with the court. Their court-appointed attorneys asked for separate trials. As the younger of the two, George was to be tried first. Sadly, also on the 13th, Newell Varno died of his wounds at Champlain Valley Hospital. When told of this news in the cell that he was sharing with his brother George, Joseph Liberty simply said, "That's bad."

Newell Varno was a Civil War veteran. He had survived the bloodiest conflict in the history of the United States and been honorably discharged. It was a tragic twist of fate that he was gunned down by a cowardly, cold-blooded murderer in his own home.

By order of Coroner Carpenter, the next day Drs. McDonald and Arthur deGrandpre performed an autopsy on Newell in the Brown's Undertaking room. It was discovered that over two quarts of blood had accumulated in the left lung of Mr. Varno. This led the two doctors to conclude that the chest wound was fatal and that Newell's death was inevitable. His remains were taken to the home of his sister, Mrs. Lewis St. Denis who lived on Waterhouse Street in Plattsburgh. The funeral service for Newell Varno took place there at 8 a.m. the next morning.

The trial for George Liberty started on Monday, December 19, 1910. George Liberty was charged with first-degree murder punishable by death. Jury selection was the court's first order of business. Once the jury had been selected, the trial continued Tuesday, December 20. The defense attorneys for George Liberty admitted that, after his brother Joseph had opened fire on Newell Varno, George shot David as he lay in his bed. The defense pointed out that George had no previous criminal record, and that there was no pre-meditation or deliberation before the shooting.

In a surprising turn of events, George's attorneys offered a novel defense strategy. They told the packed courtroom and the jury that George suffered from "fits." After further testimony by a doctor, his defense team claimed that these were actually epileptic seizures. They claimed that during these "fits," George was unable to control himself. George was known to become irritable and ill-tempered for days after a "fit" they said. The attorneys also explained that George had suffered from one of these seizures a few days prior to the shootings and therefore could not be held responsible for his irrational behavior. They pleaded with the jury to return a verdict of not guilty of first-degree murder.

Champlain Valley Hospital located in Plattsburgh, New York, was remodeled, circa 1926. This is the site where Newell Varno lingered for ten days after being shot by Joseph Liberty. *(Courtesy Anastasia Pratt, Clinton County Historian)*

The prosecution called Frank Rivers, cousin of the Liberty brothers, to the stand. Frank told of his meeting with George at the Mullen house on Saturday evening, and of walking with George and his brother Joe. Frank said the brothers were heading toward the city, and he left them at Halsey's Corners. He then continued on to the city to spend the remainder of the evening there. Frank did notice that when saying good-bye and shaking hands, Joe had on a pair of canvas gloves with the wrists cut off.

Mrs. Jennie Bourey, a relative of George, was called next. She testified that on the night of the murder, she saw George and his brother Joe at the home of her brother Fred Rivers at about 12 o'clock midnight. At the conclusion of her testimony, John Liberty, the father of the prisoner, was then called to the stand. As John passed his son on the way to the witness stand, George paled perceptibly and gave a hasty glance into his father's face while grasping the arm of his own chair with one hand and the officer sitting beside him with his other.

Under rigid examination from the district attorney, John was forced to admit that about 11 o'clock on the night of the murder, George had told him that he and Joe had shot and probably killed two men near Shield's Corners. This was in the vicinity of where the Varnos lived. His father said George was somewhat excited when telling of the killing, and he did not appear to feel sorry about it.

On cross-examination by the defense team, John Liberty told of how George was subject to frequent headaches and fits. When describing these fits, John said that they lasted from a few minutes to an hour and a half. He added that, during these episodes George's hands and arms would twitch and his face would become distorted. John described how, for the next two or three days following a seizure, George would become irritable and quick-tempered. According to John, the last time George had a fit was about a week before the shootings. On redirect examination, John Liberty stated his son was a habitual cigarette smoker and had been for six years or more. This was about the length of time he had been subject to the epileptic seizures.

Chief of Police Conners was the next witness. He testified to being at the Varno house from late Saturday evening to about 3 o'clock Sunday morning. He described how he found David Varno dead in his bed with a wound over his right eye. He also described how he arrested George Liberty that Sunday afternoon at the home of Fred Rivers, who resided in Beekmantown. The chief related how, after bringing George into the sheriff's office and placing him under intense questioning, George admitted he had shot and killed David Varno. Conners stated that when he arrested the prisoner, he had searched him and found no revolver or murder weapon. According to Conners, George told the officer that as he and Joseph Liberty fled from the Varno home, they had thrown the murder weapons away.

James B. March, a member of the Plattsburgh police force, testified he went with Sheriff Nash to the scene of the shootings shortly after 11 o'clock on the night of the murder. They found David Varno unconscious in the house and Newell wounded at the Mouso home a short distance away. District Attorney Hogue showed Officer March some canvas gloves with the cuffs torn off. Officer Marsh identified them as the ones found at the crime scene in the Varno home.

Fred Rivers, another brother-in-law of the accused, was the next witness. He testified that he had been in the city on the evening of the murder and returned home about midnight. About ten minutes after reaching his home, Joseph and George Liberty made their appearance at his house. This testimony concluded the morning session of the court.

Coroner H. L. Carpenter was the first witness called in the afternoon session. He related the confessions made by the defendant and his brother, noting their unconcerned manner while making them. Carpenter went on to say that the Liberty brothers appeared indifferent regarding their situation, and when asked by him about securing a lawyer, they declined. Carpenter told how the brothers said they killed a man and that was all there was to it.

City Judge Boire testified he had been present in the courthouse on the Sunday the defendants were arrested. He had informed them of their right to counsel. He described asking questions as to their whereabouts on the day of the shootings. Boire testified that George and Joseph Liberty both admitted to him that they had done the shooting after an afternoon and evening of drinking. The brothers went on to say they had informed their father of the shootings later that evening.

Joseph Mouso, owner of the farm where the murder occurred, said he was awakened on that Saturday night by Newell Varno, who was sprawled on his doorstep, covered in blood, and begging for help. Newell said someone had shot his brother, David, who was back at his house in the bedroom. After medical help arrived at the Mouso home, Joseph Mouso went to the Varno home where he found David Varno wounded and unconscious. This was between 11 and 12 o'clock Saturday night.

Defense Attorney Patrick J. Tierney pointed out that the killing was admitted. Tierney explained that murder in the first degree is the premeditated killing of a human being. He said no one should be punished for more than he had done. According to Tierney, his client was not responsible due to the fact he was afflicted by epilepsy. He pointed out that George was not insane at the time of the killing, but owing to the effect of epileptic fits, he was unable to decide between right and wrong. The defense then called to the stand Frank Loughlin, Milo Randall, John Noonan, and Bert Paro, who all testified to the good reputation and work ethic exhibited by the defendant during their experiences with him.

Mrs. Fred Rivers, sister of the defendant, testified that George Liberty had been subject to fits for five or six years. She said that after one of his fits last July, the defendant didn't recognize people for some time afterwards. She also testified the defendant's aunt was subject to the same kind of fits as George was.

On cross-examination, Mrs. Rivers testified that the defendant never struck or attacked anyone while suffering from one of these fits. She also stated that, to her knowledge, George had never been treated by a physician for any of the seizures.

Israel Rouger, the next defense witness, said he had seen the defendant suffering from two "fits" at the home of Fred Rivers, George Liberty's brother-in-law. Each fit had lasted about half an hour. Afterwards, the defendant did not recognize anyone.

The next three witnesses called by Tierney each stated that they had witnessed George having fits in their presence. They all agreed he was not aware of the people around him or his circumstances for a time after the fits.

Clinton County Attorney Arthur Hogue then read a statement given by Newell Varno before he died. In his statement, Varno said the Libertys had come to his home that fatal Saturday night shortly after he had gone to bed. He had risen and let them in. After they talked for a while, the brothers stood up to go.

Newell's statement said that the short one (Joseph) shot him while the other went in and shot David. Newell started for his gun and was shot a second time. The boys then ran away when Newell got his gun. Newell said he then managed to drag himself to Mouso's home where he fell, fainting on Mouso's doorstep.

George Liberty, the accused murderer, was sworn in and called to the stand by his attorney. Patrick J. Tierney had George describe his version of the "fits," including the headaches after each one. The defendant testified that he and his brother Joe had been drinking liquor that evening. He also admitted to owning a revolver. He said he had purchased it about three months earlier in order to shoot a dog.

According to George's testimony, on the night of the shooting, George and his brother each drank a pint of whiskey while on their way from Halsey's Corners to the Varno home. George's testimony varied from Newell's statement. According to George, while they were in the house, Newell went into his bedroom and placed something near the door. A little later Newell told the boys to leave, or he would help them out. George stated that as Newell said this, he was making a move toward his bedroom. That was when Joe shot him. After a second shot, George heard the bed in David Varno's room squeak. Fearing that David would come out, he went into the doorway, extended his arm, and shot David.

On cross-examination by the prosecution, George Liberty admitted that Newell was sitting in a chair to the right of Joe when Joe shot him in the face. He also admitted it was then, not earlier, that Newell started after his gun. George said that after the shootings they ran out of the house. As they fled across some fields, they threw their revolvers away. After this dramatic testimony, court was adjourned until 9 a.m. Wednesday morning.

The first witness called Wednesday morning was Dr. W. S. Buck, who was sworn in as an expert in epilepsy and its effect upon the mind. On cross-examination, the witness was forced to admit that he knew of many persons afflicted with epilepsy who operated large businesses, and did so successfully. He also admitted that from his observation of the accused while on the witness stand on Tuesday, George was responsible and knew the nature of his acts, at least at that time. Dr. T. J. Cummins was next to be called by the defense. He was presented as an expert on a person's mental and physical condition. Cummins judged that, from the testimony of the defense witnesses and doctors the accused was "of a remarkable low order of mankind." This closed the defense side of the case.

District Attorney Hogue then called John Mullen in for rebuttal. John stated that when George Liberty was at his house to hire a rig on December 3, he appeared perfectly rational. Chief of Police Conners testified that the prisoner had, in his presence and hearing, told Judge V. F. Boire on December 4 that he went to the Varno house for the purpose of killing the Varnos. Dr. E. E. Larkin testified that from his observation of Liberty on the witness stand, George was perfectly sane and that he did not have even the earmarks of an epileptic. Dr. Larkin furthered that he considered Liberty remarkable, bright and clear for one from his station in life. Dr. Larkin then gave his description of epilepsy and the effects upon the mind of the disease in long-continued cases.

Dr. McDonald, who had six years experience in the treatment of insanity at the state asylum for insane criminals at Dannemora, was the next witness. He said he observed Liberty very closely while on the witness stand. In his opinion, George was perfectly sane, and his act in the shooting of David Varno was not the action of an insane man. At 10:15 a.m., the announcement was made that the evidence on both sides was all

The Administration Building at Dannemora State Hospital for insane criminals at Dannemora, N.Y., circa 1900. *(Courtesy Pete Light)*

before the court. After a five-minute recess, Royal Corbin began to sum up the case on behalf of the accused. He said the defense had admitted to the killing of David Varno, but held the act was not that of a rational person. He made an eloquent plea on behalf of his client, asking that the jury take into consideration the fact that the boy was a victim of epileptic fits and therefore not responsible for his actions at times. Defense Attorney Tierney reiterated that Liberty was a below-average man in mental caliber, as shown by the physicians who had made a thorough examination of his mental and physical condition on Tuesday evening.

Mr. Corbin closed his plea at 11:55 a.m. and was followed by District Attorney Hogue. For forty minutes Hogue implored the jury to put aside all sympathy and return a verdict in accordance with the evidence in the case. Hogue briefly recounted the story of the heartless crime and asked that the guilty parties be punished for it. He reminded the jury that as a part of the court, they had sworn to perform their duty. As jurors their sole duty was to say whether or not the prisoner had been proven guilty of the crime with which he was charged.

Judge Kellog took half an hour in charging the jury. He explained to them the different degrees of murder and manslaughter. The judge outlined that if, in the opinion of the jury, the crime charged in the indictment had not been proven beyond a reasonable doubt, the prisoner was entitled to the jury returning a verdict of guilty to a lower degree of murder than the one for which he was placed on trial.

At the close of the instructions to the jury, Defense Attorney Patrick Tierney asked the court to charge that in case the jury found no deliberation by George Liberty was evident, he should not be convicted of murder in the first degree. The court agreed to do as requested. At 1:15 p.m. the judge directed the officers in charge of the jury to take them to a hotel for lunch, after which they were to be locked up in the jury room to begin their deliberations.

At 2:30 p.m. the jury returned to the courtroom for further instructions from the court. Upon taking their seats in the jury box, their foreman asked for an explanation of the modified murder charge requested by Attorney Tierney. Judge Kellog described to them in great detail how they could arrive at a lesser charge instead of the first-degree murder charge. They then retired to the jury room. At 6 o'clock members of the jury were still of different minds as to what their verdict should be, so the court

The Clinton County Courthouse seen on the right of the Cumberland House, where the jury in George Liberty's trial recessed for lunch and dinner on December 21, 1910. *(Courtesy Anastasia Pratt, Clinton County Historian)*

directed that they be furnished with another meal at the expense of the county. Two officers escorted the jury members to the nearby Cumberland House for dinner.

At 12:25 a.m. on Thursday morning, December 22, the foreman of the jury informed the officer in charge that they had reached a verdict. Justice Kellog was contacted as well as the defense and district attorneys and their teams. Court was reconvened at about 2:15 a.m. After the jury was seated and the prisoner brought into the courtroom, the foreman, James H. Davis, announced they had found George Liberty guilty of second-degree murder.

The lower verdict was a surprise to the vast majority of those who had listened to the evidence produced upon the witness stand and throughout the trial. The court observers believed that, to safeguard the general public, the prisoner should have been convicted of the crime for which he was charged.

There was no change in Liberty's demeanor as he heard the verdict that would save him from death by electricity. He stood stoically and did not flinch at the thought of being in prison for 20 years. This decision would make it possible for him to regain his freedom when he would be 38 years of age, still a relatively young man.

After the announcement, Patrick Tierney asked that the sentence not be passed upon the prisoner until later Thursday in order to give him time to prepare any motions he might decide to make. The judge, in compliance with this request, stated that he would defer sentence until 9 o'clock Thursday morning until which time court was adjourned.

In relating the process the jury went through to reach their decision, it was evident from the outset that they were far from any agreement of the charges. On their first ballot, the jury voted six for murder in the first degree, five for murder in the second degree, and one juror opted for manslaughter. There was a constant give and take of jurors who supported first- or second-degree murder. On the second ballot, the supporter of the manslaughter charge sided with the supporters of second-degree murder. This juror kept changing his vote for many hours. Approaching midnight, the last of the supporters of murder in the first degree were convinced to swing over to the side of the jurors who favored a second-degree-murder verdict. It was later revealed that the juror who was originally for manslaughter only changed his vote with the belief the accused would go to prison for life without the possibility of parole.

On the morning of December 22 at 9:45 a.m., the jury once again confirmed their verdict, this time before a stunned courtroom that was now overflowing with public spectators. Indignation echoed throughout the court as the verdict was read, convicting George Liberty of second-degree murder, not first-degree as charged. Through the efforts of a very competent defense team, George was saved from the death penalty.

Judge Kellog said that the jury found there was no deliberation or premeditation on the part of the defendant. With their determination, the court must be satisfied with their judgment. He then sentenced George Liberty to Clinton Prison in the town of Dannemora for a term of 20 years to life. Liberty was informed that it would be possible that, with good behavior, he could be released at the expiration of the 20-year term. Being granted that release would depend entirely on his actions.

Joseph Liberty was sitting near his brother. At a nod from him, Defense Attorney P.J. Tierney then arose and announced that Joseph was willing, with the consent of the court and district attorney, to change his

Clinton County Courthouse, Plattsburgh, New York, December 22, 1910. As George and Joseph Liberty were sentenced to Clinton Prison, hundreds of people overflowed the courthouse and grounds. *(Courtesy Anastasia Pratt, Clinton County Historian)*

plea of not guilty in the first degree to one of guilty of murder in the second degree. District Attorney Arthur Hogue stated that, considering the verdict in the case of George Liberty and there were possible elements of the case against Joseph Liberty regarding pre-meditation that may not be proven, he was willing to accept the plea for the lesser crime. The court agreed to the motion, and the clerk entered a plea of second-degree murder against Joseph Liberty. Upon the plea of guilty, Joseph was also sentenced to the same 20 years to life as his brother. He was ordered to serve his time in Clinton Prison with his brother George.

The courtroom, which had erupted into indignation at the verdict for George Liberty, became even more raucous upon the plea and sentencing of his brother Joseph. Most observers felt the verdict and sentencing were a miscarriage of justice. They feared this verdict would send a message to criminals that they could be involved in the most cold-blooded of killings in Clinton County and would not have to worry about a conviction of first-degree murder and the death penalty.

That afternoon, as the Liberty brothers were taken to serve their time at Clinton Prison by Sheriff Nash and Deputy Sheriff Stillwell, the two brothers exhibited the same utter lack of remorse and light-hearted manner that they had shown from the time of their arrest and during the trial.

Clinton prison, located in the town of Dannemora, was a maximum-security facility that had become known as "Little Siberia." It is located approximately 15 miles west of Plattsburgh. It was originally construct-ed in 1844 to house prisoners who were put to work mining iron ore in nearby Lyon Mountain. Mining continued until 1877, when the inmates started to perform various jobs and duties around the prison itself. Gen-eral maintenance and operation of the prison farm included building roads, clearing brush, and maintaining a vegetable garden.

From the time of their incarceration, George was determined to get an education and strove to make himself a better person who could, upon release, contribute to society. Joseph however, was very uncooperative and irresponsible. He made no effort to change his ways, or change the behavior that had put him in this predicament.

The Clinton County Courthouse where the Liberty brothers were tried and sentenced in downtown Plattsburgh, New York, circa 1910. *(Courtesy Pete Light)*

Almost ten years later, on November 30, 1920, Joseph Liberty was transferred to Auburn Prison in central New York State at the end of the Finger Lakes in Cayuga County. This prison had a national reputation for the strict punishment and severe treatment of its inmates. The prison's system of punishment had become known as the "Auburn system."

After serving 19 months at Auburn Prison, Joseph Liberty worked his way up to becoming a trustee. He worked outside the prison walls, serving as a cook with a road crew at the Montezuma work camp located about 12 miles northwest of Auburn. As the noon whistle sounded on July 25, 1922, Joseph Liberty escaped.

A reward of $50 dollars ($700 in 2014 money) was posted on Joseph. On the chance he would try to return to that location, officials in the Plattsburgh area were contacted and told to be on the lookout for him. But as the days and weeks passed, it became clear Liberty would not soon be recaptured or returned to the New York penal system.

In order to elude law enforcement officials, Joseph initially fled to New York City. There, he worked as a cook and a longshoreman using various aliases. After awhile, he continued west to Pittsburgh. He worked on a paving crew and eventually in a box factory.

Amid growing concerns that he would be caught and returned to prison, Joseph continued on to Chicago, and eventually went as far west as California. Soon, Joseph moved on once again. This time he went to the state of Wyoming and, after a brief stay there, he decided to take his chances and returned to New York City.

When some people he knew recognized him, Liberty went back out west to Wyoming. Co-workers knew him as "Frank Johnson." Around this time, he worked on an oil rig and for some local farmers. After more than seven years on the run, Joseph Liberty changed his name to Frank Robideau, and he settled in the Wheat Basin area of Montana, where he married May Dietzel. According to the U. S. census of 1930, he had listed his birthplace as Wyoming.

Joseph's brother took an altogether different route. He achieved his freedom through legal means. On January 13, 1924, New York Governor Al Smith commuted the sentence of George Liberty to 13 years and 25 days so that he could be released from Clinton Prison on parole. It was reported that Judge Kellog, who had presided at his murder trial, and

District Attorney Arthur Hogue, who prosecuted the case, also favored clemency. Governor Smith pointed out that the commutation of George Liberty's sentence was due entirely to reports of the remarkable change he had exhibited in educating himself and becoming a model prisoner.

An Earlier Miscarriage of Justice

George Liberty (Frank Robideau's brother)

As outrageous as the sentence of George Liberty was in the cold-blooded slaying of David Varno, his defense team did an effective job pointing out that George had a medical affliction that rendered him incapable of being responsible for his judgment at times. The defense team successfully played on the sympathy of a few jurors that were able to convince the other jurors to opt for second-degree murder rather that of first-degree murder. The jury also seemed to have a hard time distinguishing the different degrees of murder and the punishment that was given accordingly. Because of this confusion and their final decision, George Liberty received a lesser sentence that few in the community thought possible.

Joseph Liberty aka Frank Robideau

Joseph Liberty's sentence was even more outlandish. Joseph had gunned down Newell Varno with absolutely "no provocation," expressing no remorse. Joseph, aka Frank, was the key person in the killings and was the first to open fire at the Varno home. Seconds later George followed his brother's actions, going to the bedroom and shooting the other Varno brother.

Later, when asked of their motive, neither would admit it was robbery. Joseph made the statement: "We shot the old men for the fun of it."

The citizens of Plattsburgh were outraged when Joseph managed to get the same sentence as his younger brother, especially when the evidence showed that Joseph seemed to be the leader of the two. These killings sent a strong message to the community that, in the most vicious of murders, their court system was more than willing to take the easy way out – which they did.

The defense team was very strategic in trying George first, because of his younger age and supposed medical condition.

In spite of the aggressive and violent actions of Joseph, the defense attorneys plea bargained his charge down. Joseph did not even have to take the stand or face the county attorney's questioning or scrutiny of a jury.

The demeanor exhibited by Joseph Liberty and his self-serving manner did not change in prison. It led him to be transferred to a second maximum security prison. After his escape from a road crew, he crisscrossed the country using various aliases.

The internal rage that Joseph must have carried with him on a daily basis led him to commit further acts of brutal violence with little or no regard for those whom he murdered or for the consequences of their families. When Joseph first came to the Wheat Basin area in about 1929, he was still known as Frank Johnson, who had worked on an oil rig in Wyoming.

A local farmer, Emil Melby, recalled that early one morning Robideau/Liberty returned to his ranch and, in an excited state, said that he had been robbed in Billings the night before and was forced to walk all the way back to the ranch (about 35 miles). The *Billings Gazette* carried a story that a taxi cab driver had been murdered a few miles west of Billings the same night that Robideau/Liberty had been walking back to the Melby ranch. Although the crime was never solved, it was known that the bullet used in the killing of the taxi driver was from a .38 caliber – the same type of weapon used to kill the Kuntzs nearly eight years later. Frank Robideau was in the area at the time.

The plea-bargain in Plattsburgh, New York, many years earlier was egregious. It shows the dangers when attorneys and judges take the easy way out, making deals to avoid doing their job.

The case of Joseph Liberty, aka Frank Robideau, should have gone to trial as the evidence was strong and abundant. He was a vicious killer who, after committing his first murder, should never have been plea-bargained. This is also an example of law enforcement officers who were dedicated and understanding. The deaths of Mike and Frieda and the attempted killing of their son, fell directly on the discretion of the courts and the plea-bargaining system, which in this case was misused.

Chapter Eight
The Pre Trial

On Saturday, December 11, 1937, at 3:00 p.m. in the Stillwater County Courthouse in Columbus, Montana, Frank Robideau shocked everyone by changing his plea of not guilty to guilty of first-degree murder. Frank admitted that he killed Mike Kuntz in cold blood. However, he claimed that Frieda Kuntz was shot in an act of self-defense. According to Frank, when she tried to get the gun away from him, Frieda had bitten his hand so hard that Frank was forced to shoot her.

Many people in the area did not attend this hearing, as they had expected Robideau to profess his innocence. They assumed that the procedures would be long and drawn out. With the expectation of a trial by jury, the thinking was that determining the dates for the trial would probably dominate the entire process that day. Consequently, only court officials and four witnesses called by the county attorney at the request of the district judge were in the court when Robideau admitted the killing of the Kuntz couple. With his attorneys sitting by his side at a nearby table, Robideau burst into tears as they presented his case. This was the first outpouring of any emotion seen in public by the now-admitted killer.

The following are the transcripts from the Stillwater County Courthouse records. They are now in the Museum of the Beartooths in Columbus, Montana. Robideau was on trial for his life. Some of the information that his attorneys presented was Robideau's version of what had happened. His account contains half-truths or out-and-out blatant lies. However, the transcripts are very interesting and show the desperate circumstance that Robideau had created, and how they brought out the worst in him.

Opening Statement for the Pre-Trial of Frank Robideau, [Joseph Liberty], Defendant:

Chapter Eight – The Pre Trial

M. L. Parcells, Attorney:

The man whom your Honor has directed Mr. Blenkner and myself to represent before this tribunal, by his plea of "guilty" to the offense charged in the information here, places in your hands the greatest treasure which is given to man on this earth to possess, his own life, together with the right to do with it as you may see fit.

By your judgment, you will determine whether the defendant shall live out the time allotted to him by his Maker, or die upon a scaffold in expiration of the crime which, by his plea, he has admitted he committed.

For the act itself to which the defendant has pleaded guilty, we offer no defense or excuse, nor seek to condone. However, we feel we would be remiss in our sworn duty to our client by order of this Court if we did not acquaint Your Honor with such information and every fact and circumstance which we have been able to gather in the limited time at our disposal before you are called upon to assume the responsibility of acting upon a matter of such importance.

In the first place, Joseph Liberty [aka Frank Robideau], who now stands before you, and the matter of whose life or death is now in your hands, may have likewise been sinned against to such an extent as to, in a measure, entitle him to at least a prayerful consideration by Your Honor.

As we understand it, the question to be determined by Your Honor is not what you or I might have done if in his place when we look at the matter from our point of vantage at this distance, but rather as prescribed by the law, as laid down in this courtroom by one of your distinguished predecessors when he said:

"Standing where he stood, hearing what he heard, seeing what he saw and knowing what he knew, what would an ordinarily prudent man have done?"

This same Jurist even went farther and took the position that the command of the law of the State of Montana extends and applies to a Judge as well as a jury and requires the Judge to find to the defendant the same benefit of doubt on questions of fact to be determined by him.

The defendant tells us he came to the dry-land farming section of Stillwater County approximately fifteen years ago, determined to live down his past record and lead a useful, upright and moral life and, so far as the records show or we have been able to ascertain, from that time up to the commission of this act he did so. He married a lady of the Lake Basin country, May Dietzel, now twenty-six years of age, to which union three children have been born, Florence Darlene, seven, Richard Henry, five and Cleo Jane, two, and another is now expected between this date and Christmas.

Your Honor knows of his own knowledge something of the trials and tribulations of our dry-land farmers the past few years and particularly during the time since the defendant came to Stillwater County, with poor, poorer and no crops, poor and poorer prices, drought, grasshoppers and hail, but you do not know what it means to see the wife of your bosom and children of your own blood showing effects of malnutrition, suffering the pangs of hunger, staring you in the face on Thanks-giving Day, with no legal means known to you by which you could appease that hunger other than sending them to the neighbors where they could get a meal of victuals and, with the feeling in your heart, that this condition was brought about solely by the wrongful acts of another who had the means and ability to correct it if he so desired.

The defendant tells us and, so far as we have been able to check such statements, they are verified by the records and facts, that this particular trouble between the defendant and Mr. Kuntz originated in connection with the attempt of Mr. Kuntz to assist the defendant in righting what he considered a wrong, whether that wrong was fancied or otherwise, against the J. I. Case Company, from whom the defendant had purchased farm machinery from time to time since January 9, 1932, and given mortgages on the machinery and his expected crops to secure payment of the same.

On September 16, 1936, he had given that company a chattel mortgage for $500.00 covering one-half of his share in the next maturing crop of wheat on sections twenty-seven and thirty-three in township three north of range twenty-two, Stillwater County, Montana, near Wheat Basin, and on the very same day that mortgage was given, the Company repossessed every piece of machinery he had purchased from them and left him without plow, harrow, drill, tractor or combine with which to continue his farming operations. Prior to this, he had purchased eight hundred acres of land under crop-payment contract, by which he was to give one-half of the crop to be delivered in the elevator free of expenses of production, harvesting, etc., which meant that out of his one-fourth left after this mortgage, he would have to pay all expenses of preparing the ground, seeding the land, harvesting the crop, prepare and seed the land for the next crop, pay his interest and taxes, and support his wife and family for at least 12 months.

He had only about three hundred acres of dry-land wheat and, with the crops which we have been harvesting of late years in the Basin country, it just simply could not be done.

He took over the agency of the Zanol Products in order to augment his earnings in his effort to properly support his family, and so conducted his business that he was on the Honor Roll with that concern. In connection with this work, he required an automobile with which to get over the country and transport and deliver his products. Inasmuch as he had a fair prospect for crop in the year 1937, about July 8th of that year he traded in his old Chevrolet automobile on a new Dodge pickup for which he received a credit of $150.00 on the purchase price of $675.00, but which with the finance charges for extended payments amounted to $760.00. In this connection, he also gave his personal note for $75.00 to make up the increased amount.

He was unfortunate in that a hail storm came along and took about seventy-five per cent of a large portion of his wheat, with the result that he threshed something less than six bushels per acre, or approximately one thousand eight hundred bushels. The machinery company having repossessed his combine, he was compelled to hire his entire crop harvested, at a heavy expense to himself.

Chapter Eight – The Pre Trial

In order to make the monthly payments of $27.85 on this pickup, he sold to the Occident Elevator Company through the deceased as local agent for that Company at Wheat Basin, Montana, some of the wheat which he harvested, having the checks made therefore in the name of the parties who had sold him this pickup. This diversion was afterwards discovered, payment on the check stopped and the car repossessed by the finance company although he subsequently made arrangements to have it returned to him by payment of the delinquency and expenses of the repossession.

While this has nothing to do with the case before the Court except to show the nature and disposition of these different outfits who are "farming the farmer," I might state the amount due on this pickup had been reduced to $250.65, but immediately after the arrest of the defendant the finance company seized the property under their contract and proceeded to immediately sell same at another profit because of the non-payment of the monthly installment of $27.85 which he was unable to make due to his incarceration and which he tells us was verbally extended to November 28, 1937.

We fully agree with the maxim that two wrongs do not make a right, but the defendant, whether rightfully or wrongfully, claims to have actually believed he had been wronged by the machinery company and with the help of the deceased, undertook to right the alleged wrong by selling this wheat in the name of the automobile dealers, and a portion in the name of George Phillips, a fictitious person, the wheat being delivered to the elevator operated by deceased by this defendant and the checks for same likewise delivered to and cashed by defendant.

In addition to these diversions, there was one hundred-eighty bushels, and twenty pounds of wheat, according to the figures of defendant which he had delivered to the elevator run by the deceased, for which no scale tickets were ever made or evidence of delivery given to defendant by deceased or the elevator company which he represented as local agent at Wheat Basin.

The defendant tells us that he had but two or three dollars in his pocket and a shipment of the Zanol products coming in for which he did not have sufficient funds to take up the freight thereon, amounting to something like ten or twelve dollars, and went to the toilet when the express man, Mr. Fred Sheets, showed up with the consignment. That on the day following Thanksgiving, he went to the elevator about four o'clock in the afternoon to get settlement for this one hundred-eighty bushel twenty pounds of wheat, but was advised by the deceased that he, the deceased, had been getting in bad with his company on account of the former transactions and diversions, and before he would make an exposure of this additional wheat, he would blow the head off the defendant and accentuated his remarks by drawing a new automatic from the pocket of his coveralls and pointing it at the defendant, who at that time was not armed. Whether or not this statement is true, only God above with the all-seeing eye knows. The defendant says further that when the deceased refused to make payment for the wheat, he asked the deceased to let him have at least ten dollars so he could get these Zanol products for sale and distribution and in that way get something with which to support his family, which request was likewise refused.

It will be remembered that, if the statement of the defendant is true, this one hundred-eighty bushel and twenty pounds of wheat represented the only source of living for the defendant, his wife, his three children and the one expected, which the sheriff tells me had not yet been provided with clothing, and that these proceeds with what he could receive from sale of the Zanol products, would have to sustain them from that time until if, as, and when another crop could be produced, harvested and marketed.

He advises that upon all of his requests in this respect having been denied by the deceased, and in view of the threatening attitude of the deceased, the defendant went to his home and got his gun, and subsequently returned to a point behind a string of box cars near the elevator, from which he challenged the deceased to come out and "shoot it out."

The deceased refused and the defendant returned to his own home and ate a little of what there was to be had and washed the dishes and the deceased drove by in his car on the way to his home nearby, presumably for his supper.

By this time it was dark and the deceased, with his wife and boy in the car, drove back to the residence of the defendant and stopped; that the defendant, believing he had changed his mind, went out and after some conversation took place between the three of them, the deceased told the defendant to get in the car and they would go over to the elevator and he would pay the defendant for the wheat. Mrs. Kuntz apparently took the side of the defendant in the argument as to payment for this wheat and suggested to the deceased that he pay the defendant for the wheat or let him have the wheat, as she knew how hard up they were and how badly the family needed the money; that they (Kuntz) had been hard up themselves, but never anything like the family of the defendant. Then the defendant got in the car and they drove to the elevator and, after they looked over the list of names posted with the elevator company as mortgagers of crops, they picked out the names of certain local people whose crops were not mortgaged, and the deceased made out checks in their names for certain money, but not enough to cover payment for the whole one hundred eighty-bushels and twenty pounds of wheat which the defendant believed rightfully belonged to him or rather his wife, to whom he had given bills of sale for a share of the crops for the years 1934,1935, and 1936, all of which were of record in the office of the county clerk and recorded here. That when these checks were written, instead of delivering them to the defendant, the deceased folded them up and put them in his pocket, and they went out and got in the car in which Mrs. Kuntz and the boy were waiting, and proceeded to the home of the defendant, where they stopped; then the defendant started to get out of the car, and the deceased told him to "stay in" and started to drive along the road toward Columbus.

Mrs. Kuntz then asked the deceased where he was going, and her husband Mike replied to Columbus. She then asked him what for, to which he made no reply. The defendant then states they drove toward Columbus with him sitting in the rear seat of the car and the Kuntz family in the front seat with the boy sleeping between them, to the point where the crime was committed. That was when the deceased stopped the car. Mrs. Kuntz inquired why he had stopped, to which the deceased made no reply other than to say, "We will shoot it out."

That believing the deceased still had the automatic which he had seen him have in the afternoon, and momentarily expecting a bullet from same, the defendant fired the fatal shot; that he had no intention at any time of doing anything to injure Mrs.

Kuntz or the boy but that, after the deceased had been shot, Mrs. Kuntz grabbed hold of the gun and, in her effort to pull it from the grasp of the defendant, the same was accidentally discharged; that the two bodies were then in the front seat of the automobile and, as he moved that of Mrs. Kuntz to the back seat, the boy, who up to the time of the firing of the first shot had been sound asleep, seized or struck the defendant from behind and, without knowing what or who it was but assuming it was the deceased and that he had only been stunned by the shot, struck blindly with the clubbed gun, hitting the child; that the defendant had nothing but the friendliest feeling for Mrs. Kuntz, with whom he had arranged to take care of Mrs. Robideau in her coming confinement, and the boy, who was the playmate of, and about the same age as his own son; that after striking what proved to be the boy, he thought him dead, and returned the car with the three bodies in it to the elevator at Wheat Basin where it was subsequently found after the boy recovered consciousness and went to the store at Wheat Basin.

That by his faith and trust placed in Your Honor and plea of guilty in this case, the defendant has saved the taxpayers of Stillwater County thousands of dollars; that if it is the will of God to be expressed through Your Honor and the judgment of this Court, that his life be taken and his children, Florence Darlene, Richard Henry and Cleo Jane, and the child yet unborn, be further stigmatized with the fact their father was "hanged by the neck until dead."

He is ready to make the supreme sacrifice, but we respectfully submit that in view of all the facts and circumstances, during this festive holiday season, justice as to those left behind should be tempered with mercy and the old law of "an eye for an eye and a tooth for a tooth" give place to the new law promulgated by Christ during his stay here on earth.

Frank Robideau, being first duly sworn deposes and says that after due consideration he desires to make a statement of his connection with the murder of Mike Kuntz and his wife and the wounding of the Kuntz child on the 26th day of November, 1937, in Stillwater County, Montana.

That he had a quarrel with Mike Kuntz over the payment to him by Kuntz for certain wheat in the elevator managed by Mr. Kuntz. That there was a dispute over the title to the wheat and Kuntz refused to pay him for the wheat because of the claims of other persons. That he, Robideau, was in urgent need of money and insisted that Kuntz pay him for the wheat in his own name and a quarrel ensued in which Kuntz drew a gun on Robideau. That he went home to his house and got his gun, a .38 caliber revolver, and waited for Kuntz on his way home and Kuntz did not come, but later came to Robideau's house when he was cooking supper and they then agreed to go out some place and shoot it out. That it was agreed they should go in the Kuntz car and Kuntz was to drive any place he wanted to, and Kuntz drove with Robideau and the Kuntz family toward Columbus and about fourteen miles out Kuntz got so overcome or yellow that he could drive no further and Robideau said, "Is this where you want to go?" and Kuntz said shoot. Robideau then shot Kuntz through the head from the rear seat of the car, and Mrs. Kuntz grabbed his hand and held it to her breast and he pulled the trigger. That he then struck the child at the place of the shooting and drove back with the bodies and drove the car into the elevator at Wheat Basin. That he did not know whether Kuntz had his gun. He did not see him pull it but thought or supposed he had his gun with him.

After this statement from the lawyers, Dr. William Smith testified on behalf of the prosecution he felt that the child, Larry, narrowly escaped the fate of his parents. In his testimony he pointed out an injured thumb as a factor that had saved his life, as he had been struck on the head a number of times. The little boy had apparently attempted to save himself by throwing his hands over his head to ward off the blows from the butt of the gun. Some of these blows were deflected by the defensive moves of little Larry. In one of the wounds, the doctor testified that he had found a small fragment of wood, which he believed was a portion broken from the revolver stock.

At the conclusion of the testimony of Robideau's attorneys and Dr. Smith, the prosecution witness, Judge Ben Harwood set a sentencing date of December 15, 1937 at 2 o'clock in the afternoon. The proceedings that day had begun at 3 p.m. and court was adjourned at 5:30 p.m.

With the entire area in a frenzy over the killings of the Kuntz couple and severe beating of little Larry, people throughout the region were anxious for the court's decision. The *Billings Gazette* reported that Stillwater County Attorney P. R. Heily said he would ask the district judge "to impose the supreme penalty, that of hanging for first-degree murder, and nothing else."

Four days later, a tired and haggard-looking Frank Robideau was taken from his cell at the Stillwater County Courthouse to appear before the court. At the request of Judge Harwood, at approximately 3 p.m., Stillwater County Attorney P. R. Heily had fingerprint expert Yellowstone County Deputy Sheriff Albert Jansen present gruesome photographs of the bodies of the slain couple as final evidence in the case.

Following a 30-minute summation of the evidence and court records, Judge Harwood pronounced the sentence of Frank Robideau, aka Joseph Liberty. The judge called this crime, "The most brutal, savage murder in the history of Montana."

As Robideau faced the judge and heard his sentence for the slaying of Mike and Frieda Kuntz and the severe beating of their young son, his eyes blinked rapidly, but he held back any sobs.

The judge's strong voice rang out, "It is the judgment of this court that you be, and hereby are, sentenced to death." The sentence called for death by hanging between the hours of 1:00 a.m. and 11:00 p.m. on January 15, 1938.

The realization of his fate soon overcame Robideau. Seconds after court was adjourned, Robideau wiped tears from his eyes and sobbed heavily as Sheriff Murphy and Undersheriff Benjamin led him from the courtroom. After his sentencing, Robideau said, "I have nothing to feel sorry about them people. Mr. and Mrs. Kuntz, they put me in this mess I'm in now."

Back at the Stillwater County Jail, Robideau said, "I'd have been better off if I had a rope around my neck years ago." He told Undersheriff Benjamin that the judge did the right thing. "I have nothing against the judge, no more than I have anything against you."

At the same time Frank Robideau's life was sentenced to end, his wife lay in the maternity ward at the Columbus Hospital, waiting to bring a new life into the world.

The road from Columbus to Wheat Basin is a 26-mile-long dirt road. In 1937, there were no car radios in police vehicles, or other means of contact other than an occasional telephone for law enforcement to use in that area. Sheriff Murphy and Undersheriff Benjamin exhibited tremendous insight and people management in their investigation. Their inquisitive nature and shared experience allowed the officers to use their diverse skills to the best advantage and kept the teams working together. The help of the sheriff's department of Yellowstone County and several constables from the township of Billings provided the experts and other needed officers. A crime so shocking it galvanized the entire area had been solved in only two days. Justice had been swift and sure.

Chapter Nine

Robideau's Jail Time

On December 24, nine days after Judge Harwood sentenced Robideau, he was sitting in his barren isolation cell in the Yellowstone County Jail in Billings when the jailer came to his cell door. Frank received a card notifying him that his wife, May, had given birth to a girl at the Columbus Hospital the previous day. The baby was named Phyllis Jane Robideau. This was the child for whom Frieda Kuntz had agreed to act as midwife.

Frank Robideau was probably numb. He had placed himself at the mercy of the court in an effort to obtain a similar sentence to the one he and his brother had received in Plattsburgh, New York, in 1910. He hoped this would allow him to be eligible for parole in 20 years and continue to stay in touch with his wife and children. He had held hopes of someday regaining his freedom. Those hopes had been dashed forever.

Instead, the court felt that this case warranted the most severe penalty the law could deliver to this cold-blooded murderer. In Montana, this meant death by hanging.

The death penalty was not common. Only five hangings had occurred since 1920. Rural Montana used a structure known as the "Galloping Gallows."

Yellowstone County Jail located in Billings, Montana, where Frank Robideau was held for "safe keeping." His isolation cell was in the basement on the lower right side of the stairs. Circa 1937. *(Courtesy Robyn G. Peterson, Yellowstone Art Museum)*

These gallows were designed for easy transport to required locations. The various counties in Eastern Montana shared the gallows.

Sheriff Murphy had the job of coordinating the events that would lead to Robideau's final walk up the 13 steps to the hangman's noose. On December 30, 1937, Sheriff Murphy put in the order to have the gallows brought to Columbus for the hanging. The scaffold was in the town of Forsyth located in Rosebud County, so he would have to arrange for it be transported to Columbus by truck.

The Kuntz family faced further strain. Mike Kuntz had a life insurance policy through his job that, at first, the insurance company refused to pay. The policy was through workman's compensation with the Hartford Accident and Indemnity Company.

A hearing was held on January 11, 1938, to determine if Mike Kuntz was killed during the performance of his duties as an employee of the Occident Grain Company. The Insurance Company claimed Mike's death was an aggravated murder. Larry's grandmother hired a lawyer from the law firm of Mackoff and Kellogg of Dickinson, North Dakota, to represent Larry at the hearing. The attorney filed a request for $6,000 compensation for the death of Larry's father. The two attorneys also took testimony from Frank Robideau on January 11, 1938, that afternoon for presentation in seeking double indemnity on the insurance policy held by Frieda Kuntz.

At the hearing, Frank told one lie after another, with reckless abandon. When the newspapers covered the hearing, they reported, "Frank Robideau, 47, who will ascend the scaffold steps at Columbus Saturday, aired a terrific struggle between himself and Mrs. Mike Kuntz minutes before the Kuntz couple was slain, in testimony presented before the state industrial accident board in the Yellowstone County jail."

The January 13, 1938, edition of the *Columbus News* printed the following article on the hearing:

> J. Burke Clements of Helena, chairman of the state industrial accident board, presided at the two-hour hearing called for the purpose of hearing Robideau's evidence as to whether or not Mike Kuntz, Wheat Basin elevator operator, was slain in the course of his employment.

> Robideau, dressed in an old brown shirt and no strings in his shoes, was questioned by insurance company attorneys and counsel for 5-year-old Larry Kuntz, sole child of the slain couple and survivor of the death ride.

Robideau reiterated his earlier story at the hearing held 50 feet from the lower isolation cell, where he was awaiting his trip to Columbus late Friday night. The newspaper went on to report the outlandish exaggerations that Frank had continued to repeat from the time of his arrest and confession up to this time. Even though he was going to hang in a few days, Frank still lied about the events that took place on November 26, 1937. He stated the following:

I went to the elevator run by Kuntz the afternoon of the affair. I asked him to pay me the money for 180 bushels and 20 pounds of wheat that I had stored in his elevator. Kuntz told me he would blow my head off and knock my whole family off the earth if I exposed the wheat deal. He pointed a gun right up to my head. It seemed the barrel was pointing right in my eyes. I needed the money badly because my wife was expecting another baby the middle of December.

After I argued with Kuntz at the elevator, I went home and got my gun and went back to the railroad track near the elevator. I hollered, "Mike, we'll have it out right here." But Kuntz didn't come out. I went back home and cooked my dinner, washed the dishes and just as I was throwing out the dishwater, I saw Mike leaving his place in his automobile. They came over to my place; Kuntz, his wife and their boy were in the front seat. I asked him, "Do you feel better now?" He didn't answer me.

Mrs. Kuntz begged her husband to give me the money for the wheat because she knew how hard up I was. But Kuntz said, "I'll be god-damned if I'll give you any money."

But then he told me to "get in here and I'll go write you out some checks." We then went to the elevator, and Kuntz wrote checks to other farmers in the area and was going to give them to me to cash. I suggested names of some farmers and he suggested others. But he put the checks in his jacket pocket.

We got back into the car and Kuntz stopped at my house. I reached for the door to open it, and Kuntz said, "Oh no, you stay in here. I'm headed for Columbus."

And there wasn't a word spoken between none of us till we got to that place (about half way between Wheat Basin and Columbus). The last mile before he stopped, he was driving all over the road.

He stopped and thrust his gun at me. I took hold of his arm. That's when the first shot was fired out of his gun. That's the bullet in the roof of the car. I brought his arm in back of his head and he hollered at his wife for help. The gun exploded again and the bullet went through the front windshield. His wife grabbed me and had me about down. Then I shot him in the back of the head. She had an awful hold on me. She also bit my finger. I took my gun, and I realized that I couldn't be released unless I shot her.

My eyes were sticked out from the pain, then I shot her and killed her. I wasn't sure if Mike Kuntz was dead, so I shot him again through his body.

The boy was standing there on the running board, hollering. I thought that I might just as well kill him, but just then, I looked into his eyes and I saw the picture of my boy. I'm glad I didn't kill him. I hit him on the head with the butt of my gun. I then drove them back to the elevator and put the car inside. I shut the elevator door and went home.

The doomed man's struggle with Mrs. Kuntz was virtually the only new angle in the case unearthed at the hearing.

In speaking of the weapon, which Robideau said was in the possession of Mike Kuntz when the slaying occurred, Robideau testified, "I've got the gun myself buried up. It's a brand new gun."

Robideau re-emphasized his earlier statement that the incident was caused by Kuntz's failure to pay him for 180 bushels of wheat held in the elevator operated by Kuntz. He testified that a local land company was to obtain one-half the crop, a machinery company one-fourth and "my wife one-fourth for us to live on."

Robideau's final words at the hearing were, "What I told you is the God's truth. It's the last statement I'm going to make."

The attorneys spent considerable time questioning Robideau on the checks made out to other Wheat Basin farmers, allegedly given by Kuntz to Robideau for payment of the wheat. After Robideau's testimony, the hearing was postponed.

Eventually the Montana Compensation Bureau determined Mike Kuntz was "in the line of duty" when he was shot down by Robideau. It was reasoned that Kuntz was at work when he attempted to reach an agreement with Robideau over 180 bushels of grain in the elevator he managed. The company paid the insurance on Larry's dad and the $6,000 was allocated to his grandmother to help pay expenses for the care of Larry. That settlement, along with the money Larry made working during the summers when he was in high school, helped to pay for his college tuition. It is unknown if the insurance policy belonging to Frieda was ever paid to Larry.

While in jail, Frank Robideau kept his attorneys busy trying to settle his quarrel with the Occident Grain Company. On December 27, 1937, Blenkner and MacFarlane wrote a letter to the company:

Attn: Mr. Jahnke

Dear Sir:

We represent Mr. Frank Robideau and we are advised by him that he had delivered to your elevator at Wheat Basin 180 bushels and 20 pounds of wheat for which he had never been paid and for which no storage tickets were ever issued. We are also advised that at one time you suggested that you intended paying the proceeds of this wheat into court and letting the various claimants litigate their rights to the money.

Will you please advise us of the status of this wheat and your attitude in the matter, so that if it should be necessary to resort to litigation, the matter can be started without delay in order that the testimony of Robideau may be taken?

Your prompt attention will be very much appreciated.

Yours very truly,

Blenkner and MacFarland

On January 10, 1938, the company responded with a receipt:

Received of E. C. Jahnke, superintendent of the Occident Elevator company, the full sum of One Hundred Twenty-five dollars in currency as full settlement of any and all claims against the said Occident Elevator Company that may exist in favor of Joseph Liberty (Alias Frank Robideau) or May Robideau (his wife) of the estate of either of them.

Attorney for Joseph Liberty
(Alias Frank Robideau)

January 18, 1938, brought this document from the law offices of Blenkner and MacFarlane:

Received of E.A. Blenkner and M.L. Parcells the sum of sixty-two and 50/100 dollars in full settlement of any and all claims against the Occident Elevator Company by reason of any and all wheat delivered to said Occident Elevator by my husband, Frank Robideau, and by him assigned to me.

Mrs. May Robideau

As a religious man, Sheriff Murphy strongly objected to the death penalty. However, he knew it was his job to get it done correctly, so he set about making sure this hanging went exactly as planned. It was the first official execution of this type ever held in Stillwater County, and Murphy hoped it would be the last.

Everything had to be just right. Sheriff Murphy oversaw the reassembly of the gallows in a county-owned metal machinery shed that he had secured for the hanging. It was located one block from Highway 10 in the 600 block of East First Avenue North. This building had been vacant for some time and was in disrepair. However, it was one of the few structures in town that would be able to accommodate the large crowd sure to attend.

A time schedule was painstakingly planned. Murphy ensured that every man on the job knew exactly what he was expected to do, and when he was to do it. The next thing Murphy set about determining was the invitations to the event. Only persons with a valid invitation would be allowed inside the building to view the hanging. Any other person without an invitation would only be able to stand outside and get whatever glimpse they could.

The Montana law of 1937 regarding executions read: "The Sheriff of the county must be present at the execution and must invite the presence of a physician, the county attorney and at least twelve reputable citizens, to be selected by him, and he shall, at the request of the defendant, permit such priests or relatives, not exceeding five, as the defendant shall name, to be present at the execution and such peace officers as he may think expedient to witness the execution. But no person other than those listed shall be permitted at the same."

Elected officials, prominent local citizens, and law officers in the vicinity, all expected to receive a special invitation to the event. Given the circumstances of the heinous crime, there were as many as 900 requests for invitations.

At least 400 people gathered around the outside of the building and as many as 375 more were crammed into the big machine shed. The number of onlookers and curiosity seekers was roughly equal to the entire population of Columbus. Some of the curious folks on the outside of the building were able to poke holes in the metal in order to witness the hanging.

The abandoned machine shed in Columbus, Montana, where the hanging took place. The car in the photo is believed to be that of Sheriff Murphy, who was inside readying the building for the arrival of the gallows in January 1938. *(Photo by Victor Murphy, courtesy Museum of the Beartooths*)

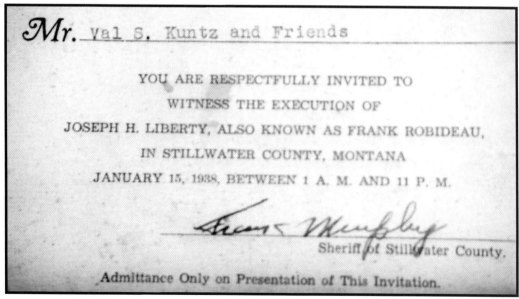

Mr. Val S. Kuntz and Friends

YOU ARE RESPECTFULLY INVITED TO

WITNESS THE EXECUTION OF

JOSEPH H. LIBERTY, ALSO KNOWN AS FRANK ROBIDEAU,

IN STILLWATER COUNTY, MONTANA

JANUARY 15, 1938, BETWEEN 1 A. M. AND 11 P. M.

Sheriff of Stillwater County.

Admittance Only on Presentation of This Invitation.

Invitation to the hanging that was sent to Val S. Kuntz, brother of Mike Kuntz. Notice the use of both names Liberty and Robideau on the invitation, signed by Sheriff Murphy. *(Hattenburg photo, Invitation courtesy Richard Kuntz.)*

Chapter Ten

The Hanging

On January 13, 1938, the *Columbus News* carried a story on the up-coming execution of Frank Robideau. It stated:

The gallows, brought in from Rosebud County and erected in the large metal shed, have been thoroughly tested by local officials. It is expected that several hundred Montana county officials, police officers and others will witness the execution.

Sheriff Murphy said that he and Benjamin will come to Billings early Friday evening and decide on what time Robideau will be taken to Columbus. He also stated that "no persons witnessing the hanging will be allowed to enter the death house with cameras, neither will anyone under the age of twenty-one be allowed access."

Robideau will be the first man to pay for a crime with his life in the history of Still-water County, which was created in 1913.

Jailer Ernest J. Oldridge of the Yellowstone County Jail was quoted saying, "Robideau has been sleeping eight to eight-and-a-half hours every night and eating lots of food three times a day."

That same day Frank Robideau ordered his last meal. It was to be served the next evening before his final ride to Columbus. The full menu for the meal was given to Sheriff Stephenson on Friday morning. Robideau ordered fried chicken, mashed potatoes, cold mince pie, and coffee.

The strain on May Robideau must have been incredible. Sheriff Murphy brought Frank's wife, May, and two of their four children to the jail for

Typically, many hangings held in the early 1900s took place at inconvenient times, such as during hours most people would have been asleep. This was done to keep the crowds to a minimum. Robideau's hanging was no exception. It took place at 1 a.m.

The "Galloping Gallows" were erected in the metal shed in prep-aration for the hanging of Frank Robideau in January 1938.
(Photo by Lloyd Maxon, courtesy Museum of the Beartooths)

a last visit at 11 a.m. Their other two children were victims of scarlet fever and were quarantined at the home of their uncle Ed Meyers near Columbus. The children had been staying there while their mother was in the hospital having her baby.

Murphy said May spoke few words on the long drive from Columbus to Billings. She appeared calm and resigned to her husband's fate. Frank's youngest daughter was three weeks old, and he was seeing her for only the second time. His oldest daughter, aged 7, accompanied her mother.

While guards stood by, Frank removed a week's beard growth with a safety razor in the jail barbershop. He just finished shaving when May and the children arrived. His noon meal was then brought in while May was there, so the jailer offered her and the children a meal as well. She thanked him for his kindness but declined, saying they were not hungry.

This final visit tested Robideau's composure. Thoughts of the family and their future, and his impending death, made the visit tough for both him and May. Officers said Mrs. Robideau and her two young daughters left the jail at 4 o'clock Thursday afternoon without a tear in their eyes.

When she left the jail, May went to visit with Coroner McColley to make arrangements for Frank's funeral. It was set for January 17 at 2 p.m. The funeral would take place at the McColley Funeral Home in Columbus, with burial following at the Mountain View Cemetery.

In a local paper, jailer Ernest J. Oldridge said, "Robideau is as composed as the day he was brought into jail. He seems stoical and has never expressed regret for his crime."

While May and her children were at the jail visiting Frank, Sheriff Murphy held a conference with Sheriff Stephenson relative to Robideau's "last ride" from Billings to Columbus. The Sheriff and other local officers would trail the automobile carrying Robideau to the Columbus machinery shed, now being called the "death house."

Rev. H. S. Tool was the only person Sheriff Dan Stephenson let visit Robideau regularly unless someone had a card from Sheriff Murphy giving them permission to see him. The reverend first visited Robideau on January 8, and returned to see him a few more times the following week. His last visits were for a short time on Friday afternoon and again for about five minutes following Robideau's last meal that evening.

According to the *Billings Gazette* on Thursday morning of January 13, any last attempt for clemency would not be forthcoming. Governor Roy E. Ayers stated that there had not been any requests from Robideau's family regarding clemency or mercy. Robideau had instructed his lawyers not to appeal to the governor for that consideration. Robideau knew that if he received a reprieve, it would mean that he would then remain in jail for the rest of his life with no possibility of parole.

"I deserve what's coming to me," he told one reporter, although he never expressed any regret for the terrible murders of Mike and Frieda Kuntz and the beating of their little boy. He also stated after his execution he would "return as a rattlesnake and bite County Attorney Heily in the butt."

Robideau requested that a reporter of the local newspaper be allowed to ride with him and the sheriffs from the jail in Billings to the gallows in Columbus. Sheriff Dan Stephenson phoned Don McCarthy of the *Billings Gazette* to ask if he would want to ride along, and Don agreed to go. McCarthy said that it would be quite the interview for the top story of the Saturday edition of his newspaper.

When McCarthy arrived at the jail around 5:30 Friday evening, a large number of people were already gathering in the front of the building. The sheriffs were telephoning their deputies stationed in Columbus at ten-minute intervals. Murphy wanted to make sure preparations were proceeding on schedule and especially wanted to check on any threat of possible crowd violence outside the hanging shed. There were some rumors of trouble that might occur upon their arrival in Columbus.

On Friday, January 14, when Sheriff Stephenson delivered Frank's last meal at 9:30 p.m., Frank said to him, "If you're born to be hung, you'll never die in a feather bed and if you're born to die in a feather bed, you'll never be hung." He then wrote a final letter to his wife and put the return address of Box 1343, Billings, Montana, office of the Billings, Montana county sheriff. He said the hardest part was saying goodbye to his wife and children. In his parting letter, he asked May to "place the letters you sent me when I was in jail on my bosom before the lid is placed on the casket. I feel sorry for you and your welfare. I was upset after you left and it is hard for me to write." He ended the letter with, "Love and kisses for you and the babies. Your husband, Frank Robideau."

Sheriff Murphy gave Robideau a blue work shirt, dark pants, and a blue coat to wear. At 11:30 p.m., he was taken from his isolation cell where he had been held since his sentencing. McCarthy watched and probably wondered what compelled this small 47-year-old man to live the life of a murderer and repetitive liar since he was at least 20 years of age.

Prior to leaving the jail, someone found the condemned man a drink of whiskey before Officer O'Donnell placed him in handcuffs. Stillwater and Yellowstone County officers hurriedly escorted him through scores of citizens who had crowded around outside the jail, attempting to get a glimpse of him. When they reached the police car, Robideau was seated in the back between Sheriff Stephenson and Undersheriff Eddie O'Donnell. They placed manacles on his ankles. Undersheriff Benjamin drove, with reporter McCarthy sitting in the front passenger seat. Sheriff Murphy and three other officers drove in a car ahead of them, and two other cars brought up the rear. The small procession proceeded on its way for the 36-mile drive to Columbus.

On that wintry night the caravan encountered a few light snow flurries, so drove to Columbus at a speed of about 25-30 miles per hour. Undersheriff Benjamin had allowed for a 90 minute drive in order to give them plenty of time to reach their destination, given the road conditions.

After they had driven several miles in an uncomfortable silence, Robideau asked Stephenson for a cigar, saying it would be the last time he would ask for one – this would be his last smoke. The sheriff then lit one for him. Each time Robideau indicated he wanted a draw on the cigar Stephenson would place it in his mouth, and then remove it when Frank nodded. A few minutes later, Frank asked for another drink of whiskey, so he could die happy. A bottle was produced from somewhere in the car. A few miles further on, Robideau nervously asked if anyone would like to flip a coin and trade places with him. No one took him up on the offer.

Frank asked Undersheriff Benjamin if there were golden steps up to the scaffold, and also added, "It would be a good idea if there were an elevator, it will be quite a walk."

Then Robideau said, "McCarthy, you are an Irishman and I love Irish songs. My last request of you is to lead us in '"My Wild Irish Rose."' Ironically, this was the song that he and his brother George had sung on their way back to jail after being identified by Newell Varno as the men who had shot him and killed his brother David 27 years earlier in New York. McCarthy started singing, and the whole group joined in as they sang the entire song. When the song was over, Robideau asked Mc-

Carthy to write a good story about him for the paper the next morning and said that "if you don't, I will come back and haunt the hell out of you tomorrow night."

A few moments later, at about 12:45 a.m., they had reached the top of the hill above Columbus and could see the lights of the town through the haze of the early January morning. Benjamin had remained in second place in the line of cars until the death caravan entered the city limits of Columbus. At that point, he sped up and passed the lead car and headed toward the machine shed. Benjamin could not help noticing the scores of automobiles parked alongside the road near the main entrance of the large metal building that would be Frank Robideau's final destination.

A deputy had been watching for them and, as Benjamin's car approached, he opened the large sliding door on the side of the building, allowing Benjamin to drive inside and park next to the gallows. In the hopes of minimizing the already tense atmosphere inside, the men who had received invitations had not been allowed to enter the building until 12:30 a.m.

Frank Murphy estimated that 30-40 highway patrolmen, sheriffs and police officers were present from various parts of Montana. Other officers from several states had also gathered to witness the hanging. Those included were Edward J. Fadring, of the San Bernadino, California Police Department, and officers from Beach, North Dakota, and Cody, Wyoming. Mike Kuntz's brother Val had come from North Dakota to witness the hanging, and he had a reserved place right in front of the gallows. Miss Florence Bowie had managed to get an invitation. She carefully disguised herself by dressing in men's clothing, and joined the large gathering of invited guests inside the machine shed. This was the first time that a woman was known to have witnessed a legal hanging in Montana.

A large crowd of at least 400 people outside the machine shed tried to see through the holes in the old metal siding where the large nails had fallen out or tried to puncture a hole of their own. Sixteen-year-old Bob Harsha was too young to get an invitation, so he stood outside in the 18-degree cold and found a hole that he could peer through to observe the event. He watched as the officers slowly removed the manacles from Robideau's ankles and handcuffed him to Officers O'Donnell and Stephenson. Harsha is the only known living eyewitness to the hanging. He remembers the emotional mix of sorrow and determination to see justice done, and the uncomfortable anticipation of the crowd that night.

Bob Harsha in his barbershop at Columbus in 2013. He stood outside the metal building and found a hole he could peer through to witness the hanging of Frank Robideau. At 94 years of age, he still cuts hair and likes to golf in his spare time. *(Courtesy Clay Scott, Mountain West Voices)*

There was hardly a sound from the crowd as the group walked the short distance to the stairway of the gallows. A solemn silence overtook the large throng of onlookers as Robideau went to his directed spot. Robideau looked the crowd over briefly, but he showed no signs of recognizing anyone as he stood at his place at the bottom of the stairs of the "Galloping Gallows."

One of the handcuffs on Robideau was removed so that he could put both hands behind his back, and he was then re-cuffed. Two heavy straps were tied around his waist to hold his arms in place. Robideau's face became pale as he looked up the stairs. Glancing at the men with whom he had ridden in the car, Robideau said, "Well, goodbye, boys."

With Undersheriff Benjamin and Deputy Paul Rosean leading the way, he rapidly climbed the 13 steps. Ascending the stairs without hesitation, he must have thought to himself how ironic it was that 27 years ago he had avoided going to the electric chair in New York, only to now be in a worn-out building in rural Montana, surrounded by a large throng of people about to witness his hanging. By his quick climb to the scaffold platform, it seemed as if Robideau was welcoming the end of the ordeal.

When Robideau reached the top, Undersheriff Ed O'Donnell bound his ankles with straps, and Undersheriff Benjamin asked Robideau if he wanted to make a last statement. Robideau took a deep breath and, glancing over the hundreds of faces in the crowd, said, "About all I wish to say is, if you have any sympathy to show, don't show it to me. Please show it to my wife and my family, as they need it. I don't need it....that's all I have to say."

In the eyes of the law, Robideau was correct in that statement. He was responsible for a senseless bloody crime in upper state New York and in eastern Montana.

After Robideau's brief statement, Deputy O'Donnell placed a black muslin hood over his forehead, pulling it down to cover his face. He then slipped the noose over Robideau's head and carefully tightened it around his neck, making sure the knot was located behind his left ear.

At 1:10 a.m. Mountain Standard Time on January 15, everyone in the crowd could hear the echo as Undersheriff Jack Benjamin snapped his fingers. This was a signal for Sheriff Frank Murphy to pull the trip cord that released the latch on the trap door of the scaffold. Robideau quickly fell from view behind the canvas skirting that had been draped from the platform to the floor. The rope went tight and swayed for a few moments, then became still. Robideau's neck had been broken.

The somber silence continued for what seemed to be an eternity as Dr. A. V. Blackstone went behind the canvas curtain. The doctor shortly re-emerged from beneath the scaffold, announcing the official death of Frank Robideau.

The court-appointed witnesses for the hanging lined up to sign the official document declaring they had observed Frank's death and his sentence pronounced by the court had been carried out. The official witnesses for the hanging were Charles Glenn, Chevy garage owner; Dr. C. H. Swanson, dentist and mayor; Bill Craig, county treasurer; Dr. George H. Payne, Columbus osteopath; and Homer E. Anderson, the high school superintendent. This completed the first court-dictated hanging in the history of Stillwater County.

Telegraph lines had been left open in order to send news to Richardton, North Dakota. Sheriff Murphy contacted the families of Mike and Frieda Kuntz, notifying them that the execution of Frank Robideau had been successfully concluded. The trauma would remain with each and every one of them, even though justice had been carried out swiftly.

The Stillwater County Coroner's Register, page 178, stated the following: Name: Frank Robideau, alias Joseph Liberty; Place of execution: Machine shed in east part of Columbus; Description of locality where body was found: Hangman's noose; Age 47, Height 5 feet 5 inches, eyes gray, dark hair, dark complexion, 130 pounds. It also listed the main witnesses to the execution: J. S. Benjamin, Deputy Sheriff; Frank Murphy, Sheriff; County Physicians W. P. Smith and A. V. Blackstone; P. R. Heiley, County Attorney; O. R. Ray McColley, County Coroner.

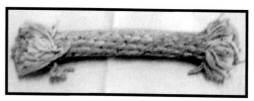

A portion of the trip cord pulled by Sheriff Murphy to release the trap door on the scaffold of the gallows. This was given to Val Kuntz by the sheriff following the hanging as a memento. *(Hattenburg photo, courtesy Richard Kuntz)*

According to the *Dickinson Press*, not only did Val Kuntz have the satisfaction of seeing the murderer of his brother and sister-in-law hanged, he brought home with him some mementos. He was given a piece of the hangman's noose, a part of the trip cord and a small piece of wood from the gallows.

Because it was only about four blocks from the hanging shed, the Atlas Bar served many spectators and local townspeople before and after the hanging. This establishment, with two stories in use at the time, served close to 600 customers. At about 3:15 that morning, owner T. P. Mulvihill announced that this was the biggest night they had ever had in Columbus.

May Robideau hired Lloyd Maxon, a local photographer, to take a photo of Frank while he lay in his coffin in the McColley Funeral Home. It is said that May hung this portrait of Frank on her living room wall for everyone to see when visiting. This was not an unusual practice at the time, as many families had no other photo or image of their ancestors who had passed on.

Frank Robideau was buried two days later in the Mountain View Cemetery in Columbus next to his three year-old son Phillip, who had died the year before from pneumonia.

On January 20, 1938, the *Columbus News* printed a "Card of Thanks" that read:

> I wish to thank those who stood by me in time of grief and sorrow during the time of death of my beloved husband, Frank Robideau.
> Sincerely yours,
> Mrs. Frank Robideau and children.

For May, this was the end of a terrible ten-week journey that must have been nerve-racking and gut-wrenching. In the short space of ten weeks, she learned that her husband was not the person he claimed to be and was a cold-blooded murderer. She had given birth and nursed two children through scarlet fever. Now, she had to see to feeding her family and burying her husband. Again, Frank, aka Joseph, had brought grief to the innocent survivors of his terrible deeds.

May and many others continued to refer to Robideau as the man they knew, not the escaped killer from New York whose given name was Joseph Liberty.

Robideau's lies continued to be investigated even after his execution. On January 16, 1938, one day after the hanging, the *Columbus News* reported Sheriff Murphy, Undersheriff Benjamin, Attorneys E. A. Blenkner, M. L. Parcells, and the Rev. H. S. Tool attempted to find the gun that Robideau said Mike Kuntz had in his possession on the night of the murders.

Robideau had told Rev. Tool, who had been his spiritual advisor during his time in jail, that the gun was hidden under a railroad tie on a section of the tracks running between the two elevators in Wheat Basin. The five men closely examined that section of the railroad, but could not find any trace of the weapon Frank stated had been hidden there.

By having the court-appointed attorneys present, and a respected "man of the cloth," Sheriff Murphy hoped to put to rest any possible controversy of an alleged weapon held by Mike. The officers were offended at the newspaper reports that hinted that Mike Kuntz was a violent man. They never placed any credence in Robideau's excuses, given the fact that he had spun so many webs of deceit and lies from the time of his arrest up until the time of his execution. However, they knew it was their duty to look, thus closing the last official chapter of this terrible tragedy.

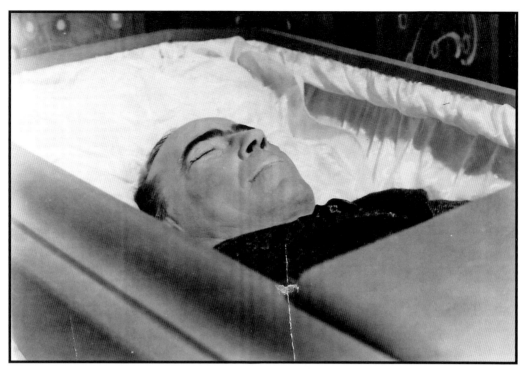

Frank Robideau, aka Joseph Liberty, in his coffin on January 17, 1938, in the McColley Funeral Home in Columbus, Montana. *(Photo by Lloyd Maxon, courtesy Museum of the Beartooths)*

Gravesite of Frank Robideau, located in the Mountain View Cemetery in Columbus, Montana. Note the incorrect year of his death, which should show 1938. *(Hattenburg photo)*

In a response to a column claiming that the hanging of Frank Robideau was cruel and unusual, Larry Kuntz's cousin, Val Kuntz, (son of Henry Kuntz) of Belgrade, Montana, wrote the following:

It seems rather odd that the columnist wanted only for us to read so much of the story depicting the side of the murderer, but never really got to the heart of the matter or the real truth about the victims. What was ignored, however, was that Mr. Robibeau was a previous offender and escaped convict from the state of New York. He came to Montana then repeated the same offense. Had he been hanged the first time, two people, in the prime of their lives, would still be alive.

Mr. Robibeau killed my uncle and his wife leaving their little boy, 5 1/2 years old, for dead by a beating with a pistol. In the back seat of a car with his dead parents, the boy came to. After attempting to awaken them, with no results, the gravely-wounded youngster crawled out of a side door of the elevator and walked to a nearby store to get help. It was there that he ran face-to-face into the murderer, in the store. The store owner took care of him instead of the killer, sparing his life.

But the boy, my cousin, was left with many unanswered and empty questions. No parents to parent him or to grow up with. What would his father have been like/or his mother as they all got older? I have no problem with the hanging. They had a job to do and they got the job done. Two innocent people were killed, forever changing the life of a little boy. Who speaks for them?

For those who are curious, the hanging method used is known as the "long drop." The other two types are the short drop and the suspension hanging. The long-drop method was designed to break the prisoner's neck by allowing them to fall a predetermined distance and then be brought up with a sharp jerk by the rope. At the end of the long drop, the body is still accelerating under force, but the head is constrained by the noose. With the knot on the noose properly placed under the left side of the jaw, the head is rotated backwards, which, combined with the momentum of the body, breaks the neck and ruptures the spinal cord, causing instant deep unconsciousness and rapid death.

Carrying out the sentence by the letter of the law as dictated by the courts, Sheriff Murphy and the officers involved properly performed a humane execution of Frank Robideau.

Chapter Eleven

No Longer a Victim

On December 9, 1937, the *Columbus News* ran the following story:

Larry Kuntz, a patient at Stillwater Hospital since Saturday, November 27, left Wednesday evening for Richardton, North Dakota, where he will make his home with his grandmother [Frieda's mother, Mary Hammerschmidt].

After twelve days in the hospital, the little boy has mended his physical wounds. He was accompanied by his aunt Genevieve Hammerschmidt, who has been with him for the last ten days. Larry, who was the only survivor of his family when his parents, Mr. and Mrs. Mike Kuntz, were murdered Friday evening, November 26, has fully recovered from the injuries that were inflicted on him that same evening.

While Larry was still in the hospital, a train took his parents' bodies to Richardton. Mike and Frieda had lived in Richardton, Antelope, and Beulah, North Dakota, before moving to Wheat Basin and were both members of large families. The *Dickinson Press* of Richardton, North Dakota, wrote that funeral services were held at 10 a.m. December 2, 1937, with Father Peter Fahreback, pastor of St. Mary's Catholic Church, officiating. Interment was at the St. Mary's Cemetery. Larry never imagined when he left North Dakota in April that this would be the way his parents would return home.

The people of the Richardton area who knew Mike and Frieda were in shock when hearing of the tragic deaths of the highly respected and beloved couple. Mike Kuntz was known to have been a quiet and peace-loving man who never carried a gun or had any kind of confrontation with another person. Many people described him as someone who enjoyed life and was always looking forward to a new adventure. They called the confession of Robideau that included Mike holding a gun a "fantastic story" and an unlikely "yarn" that could not have possibly occurred in the manner which he described.

Mike Kuntz's father had died several years before, but his mother, Mrs. Simon Kuntz, still resided in Richardton. Mike was survived by five brothers: Val, residing south of Richardton; Martin near Mott, North Dakota; Henry in Missoula, Montana; Jacob at Regent, North Dakota; and Simon in Idaho. Also, surviving Mike were four sisters: Rose (Mrs. Jacob Messer, Bowman, North Dakota); Cecilia (Mrs. John Herauf, New England, North Dakota); Eugenia (Mrs. Eugene Conion, Antelope, North Dakota); Margaret (Mrs. John Sticka, New England, North Dakota).

Mike's wife, the former Frieda Hammerschmidt, daughter of Mrs. Mary Hammerschmidt, a longtime Richardton resident, was also survived by her six sisters: Rose (Mrs. Fred Born, Jr., Richardton); Louise, (Mrs. Charles Schmidt, Richardton); Loretta (Mrs. Ray Hardy, Richardton); and Genevieve, Eleanor, and Marie, Richardton; and by two brothers: Frank and Joe. Her father, Joseph, and another sister, Florence, preceded her in death.

Now Larry was technically an orphan. However, he was fortunate to have a loving and caring extended family. Both sides of his family wanted custody of Larry, with several of his aunts and uncles offering to adopt him. The courts agreed that it would be fair for both of his parents' families to share the custody of him. It was decided that he would spend the school year with his grandmother Mary Hammerschmidt (Frieda's mother). Larry would then live with his dad's brother, Val Kuntz, and

his wife, Helen, and their children on his farm during the summer months. Their farm was located about ten miles south of Richardton. This arrangement worked out well, as both sides of the families could be with Larry during this important time of transition.

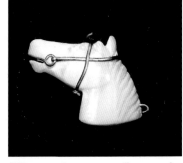

Val's land was originally homesteaded by his father, Simon Kuntz, in 1898. It is located about two miles north of the Heart River. It is also close to the place where Colonel George Armstrong Custer made camp with his troops during their ill-fated journey to the grasslands of the Little Bighorn, Montana, in 1876. Larry and his cousins Simon, Eugene, Eddie, and Richard had a great time searching for arrowheads and other treasures in the area. His un-

The ivory horse's head found by Val Kuntz on his farm. This was most likely a chess piece left by a soldier that had camped there years before. *(Courtesy Richard Kuntz, Hattenburg photo)*

cle once even found a carved ivory horse's head that one of the troopers must have had while at the campsite. By the size and shape, it looks to have been used as a chess piece.

Larry was elated to find that his Uncle Val had brought his dog Shep to live on the farm, so that he and his cousins could play with him during his time there.

Even with the solid support he got, the first few years of living with his grandma and uncle were very hard for Larry. Even though his family provided him a loving, comfortable environment, the young boy missed his mama and papa deeply and dearly.

The horrors of the murders of his parents and his own near-death were still so vivid in Larry's mind, that he was plagued by nightmares for several years. His Aunt Marie remembers reading bedtime stories every night to try to help Larry have more peaceful dreams instead of the terrifying ones that forced him to relive that ghastly experience over and over.

Larry also remembers sitting in his classroom during the school day and suddenly crying uncontrollably. When his teacher was unable to console him, she would send for Aunt Marie, who was a student at the high school in the building next door. There were times when his aunt was unable to console the little boy, so she would take him home to Grandma's house, which was only a few blocks from the school.

Grandma Mary Hammerschmidt had moved to her house in Richardton after her husband, Joseph, died of a heart attack at a young age on April 11, 1925. At the time of his death, Mary was expecting her youngest child. Joe was born in July of that same year. Trying to keep up the farm where they had been living and raise a young family by herself was just too much for Mary, so she eventually sold the farm and moved into Richardton.

Grandma worked hard at raising her family and, before long, some of her older daughters were getting married and moving out. Larry's mom had been the second daughter to do so. With this all taking place during the Great Depression, it was even more of a challenge to find work and make ends meet.

Larry remembers his grandmother going to the city hall to sew clothing with other women of all ages in order to earn some money. When

the clothing was finished, it was given to the poor. This was probably a
Works Progress Administration (WPA) project that President Franklin
Roosevelt developed to help create jobs.

Another government program the family took advantage of provided
fresh fruit and cheese for the many families who were in need. This not
only helped feed millions of people nationwide, it provided a market
for the farmers that had been hit so hard during the Depression. Larry
would pull his wagon the few blocks to city hall where the food was dis-
tributed. He especially enjoyed the grapefruit and cheese they received.

During this same time period, when our country was engaged in
World War II, many potential draftees were unable to pass their
physical examinations due to malnutrition. This led directly to the
U.S. government establishing the federal lunch program in public
schools, so the country could have a fighting force of young men ca-
pable of serving in our armed forces during time of war or a national emergency. This program was initiated by Franklin Roosevelt.

Several of his aunts had jobs with the local phone company where his
mother had worked. His Aunt Genevieve worked at a grocery store. Everyone contributed to the family during this difficult financial time, and
they made their supplies stretch, occasionally using the Sears catalog as
an uncomfortable substitute for expensive toilet paper.

One of the really great things about the location of Grandma's house
was that it was only three or four blocks to a hill that provided great
sledding during the long, cold winters. Larry and his friends spent many
Saturdays and Sundays sledding down the icy hill, stopping just short of
a pond at the bottom of the hill. This pond was where a lot of the kids in
town would go swimming during the summer months.

Larry loved to read. His favorite books were adventure novels. The Ed-
gar Rice Burroughs *Tarzan* series became Larry's favorite reading ma-
terial. He also surprised the nuns at the abbey when in grade school he
asked them to get him a book that the local library did not carry. They
could not believe he would be interested in reading *Dr. Jekyll and Mr.
Hyde*. Much to his delight and their surprise, he thoroughly enjoyed the
suspenseful novel.

One spring day, Uncle Joe Hammerschmidt took Larry to a nearby lake
for some fishing. Rising at dawn in the chilly morning, the two fisher-

Larry with his grandmother, Mary Hammerschmidt, in front of her house in Richardton, circa 1943. *(Courtesy Larry Kuntz)*

men were off for an adventure. The crappie (pronounced croppie) bite was excellent that day and, in a short period of time, they each caught their 20 fish limit. Upon returning home, the task of cleaning the catch commenced. It seemed to Larry that every time he would clean one fish, another two or three would mysteriously appear. With the process finally complete, Larry felt good that he was contributing to the family's food supply.

Larry grew to love fishing. Summer time would also find Larry and his cousins spending time fishing in the small creek that ran through their farm. With their poles made of bamboo and a string for line, they caught numerous bullheads (catfish) and suckers that were generally very small. Most of the time their hooks were simply made of bent safety pins. He and his cousins were excited when occasionally Val would present them with real fish hooks he had picked up in town. Larry didn't think the fish they caught were the best-tasting. However, his Aunt Helen would cook them, and they would eat them anyway.

During his summers on the farm, Larry and his cousins would work with his Uncle Val cutting and baling hay as well as shocking the grain during harvest season. The grain was cut and tied by machine into bundles, that were then stood on end by Larry and his cousins to dry. When put together, the bundles were called shocks. A shock was made up of 15-20 bundles of grain stalks. When the bundles had dried, they were loaded on a wagon by the Kuntz boys and taken to a threshing machine. At the thresher, the bundles were placed on a conveyer belt that carried them into the thresher, separating the grain from the straw and the chaff.

On November 16, 1943, when Larry was 11 years old, Grandma Hammerschmidt married John Schmidt. John was a retired farmer whose son had taken over his farm, which was about ten miles out of Richardton. The entire family felt fortunate to have such a loving and caring individual as John become a part of their lives. John, being the frugal person he was, would be quick to turn off the light when Larry was in bed at night reading. To satisfy his love for books, Larry kept a flashlight under the covers to continue reading in bed. John and Larry had a good relationship, and he, too, helped provide Larry with a stable, nurturing environment.

Although Larry had been fully integrated into his extended family and had a wonderful upbringing, it was not without constant heartache and sadness from missing his parents. He could not help wondering what life would have been if they were still here.

When Larry was in high school, he spent the summer of his senior year working on a county bridge crew. He enjoyed being outdoors and the money he earned was saved to help pay for some of his college tuition. He was inspired to become a pharmacist by a wonderful gentleman named John Klein, who owned the local drug store in his hometown of Richardton, North Dakota.

After graduating from Assumption Abbey High School in 1950, Larry and one of his cousins, Florence Born, were invited by their aunt Marie Stoltz to come and live with her in Spokane, Washington.

Larry Kuntz's 1950 high school graduation photo. *(Courtesy Larry Kuntz)*

By doing so, they would be able to attend Gonzaga University, as she lived near the campus. This move was also beneficial because the many streams, rivers, and lakes in the Spokane area afforded Larry some great enjoyment.

Gonzaga University did not have a pharmacy program so, after spending one year there, Larry decided to transfer to North Dakota State College (now University), in Fargo. He graduated with his pharmacy degree in 1954. Larry went on to work as a pharmacist with John Klein for a year and a half in Richardton. However, he had really enjoyed the time he spent in Spokane, so in 1956, he applied for a job at the Thrifty Drug Store located on that city's north side.

Upon his return from his interview with Larry, the owner told a young female employee named Janet Stannard, who was working in the cosmetics department, that he had just hired her future husband. A short time thereafter, that teasing statement turned out to be true. Larry and Janet began dating about a month after he started his new job. In the meantime, Larry purchased a 1957 Chevrolet convertible. One of his uncles teased Larry that he would be married before he could get it paid off. His uncle was right. In fact, Larry proposed to Janet in that car, and they were married in August of 1958.

Early on in their dating, the subject of family came up and Janet asked Larry about his relatives. He replied that his parents had been murdered when he was very young. Janet asked Larry if he remembered anything about the murders, and he replied, "Like it was yesterday."

Janet was so distraught by this answer that she decided to never ask Larry about his parents or what had happened to them again. A short time later, a cousin told her the story of Larry's parents and what had happened to them in Wheat Basin. The subject was not brought up again for another 40 years.

Larry gave Janet a ring that had belonged to his mother, and she treasures it to this day. Janet's parents were selling their house about the time they married, so Larry and Janet purchased it. It is the same house where they currently live in Spokane, Washington.

Wedding photo of Larry Kuntz and Janet Stannard in Spokane, Washington, on August 12, 1958. *(Courtesy Janet Kuntz)*

They raised four great children – three girls and one boy: Lori, Mike, Lisa, and Kristi. Their children all are grown and have careers of their own. They often have family get-togethers, game nights, and celebrations centered at the family's home base – Janet's and Larry's house.

Lori attended Eastern Washington University and, while there, enlisted in the Army ROTC program. Her military obligations took her to several states, as well as Germany for a time. She and her husband, Rick Jordan, live in Chattaroy, Washington, with their five boys. Lori is currently a surgical scheduler for a doctors group in Spokane.

Mike, named for Larry's dad, loved sports and played football at North Central High School. He received a football scholarship to Spokane Falls Community College, where he played football for one year. During the following summer, he fell from a tree, breaking his back. Mike is paralyzed from the waist down due to injuries from the fall. Despite this life-changing event, Mike still finished his electronics technician degree at the college and has worked at Huppins HiFi in Spokane for over 24 years. He lives very independently at his home in Spokane. It is known among his siblings that he is the one you want on your team in a game of trivia or tests of knowledge. He enjoys hunting and fishing.

Lisa was a cheerleader and Spokane Lilac Princess at North Central High School. She went on to attend college, becoming a surgical technician, and worked at Sacred Heart Hospital for many years. She married and has one son. Lisa currently works as an office manager for an educational software company.

Kristi also loved sports, primarily softball, and she received a college scholarship for it. She has earned several national All-American softball awards during her adult career. She is also an American Softball Association Hall of Fame member. She has worked for Spokane County Juvenile Court for 18 years and is a supervisor in the CASA/Guardian Ad Litem program, advocating for abused and neglected children.

Janet and Larry's family is very close-knit, and they are always helping each other out, as well as giving of themselves to others. Their children attribute this to the kind, generous, and giving nature of their parents. Larry's children characterize him as a very loving, easy-going, good-hearted, genuine man, who has been the anchor that holds his family together.

Larry and Janet were very active in their children's lives as they were growing up. They were members of the P.T.A., and Larry was a Boy Scout leader. Janet was very active in their school functions and never missed an athletic event or activity that the kids were involved in. One especially memorable event was when Larry and a couple of other fathers volunteered to take their scout boys on a rafting trip down the Spokane River. Larry showed up, but none of the other fathers did. He had a wild time trying to keep track of all those scouts. But Larry, true to form, did a great job, and the trip was a fun and educational time for those boys.

LARRY KUNTZ
Registered Pharmacist, graduated from North Dakota State College School of Pharmacy in 1954.

The *Spokesman-Review* in Spokane, Washington, had an article about Larry in 1975 regarding his training and work as a pharmacist. *(The Spokesman-Review)*

Larry worked as a pharmacist at various drug stores in Spokane for over 50 years before he retired. Janet worked at Garry Middle School for 24 years in the business office, until she retired. It was interesting to note that while Larry was working as a pharmacist, he was held up at gunpoint two different times. Larry was able to handle those situations in a surprisingly calm manner. He describes having immediate flashbacks to the night of his parents' murder both times the guns were pointed at him.

In 1981, Larry and a fellow pharmacist purchased the Northhill Drug Store and worked together there for 10 years, until 1991, when they sold it. After that, Larry went on to work for other pharmacies in the Spokane area, and he was so beloved and trusted by his customers that many of them would take their business along with him when he changed jobs.

Janet and Larry now keep busy with their grandchildren and great-grandchildren, taking care of their yard and keeping in touch with their many friends. Janet and Larry are avid Washington State University and Eastern Washington University football fans. Following the Gonzaga University basketball teams is also a passion of theirs. Janet often irritates Larry by listening to the games on the radio while watching the telecast on the TV. (Author Tim Hattenburg's lovely wife, Becky, can relate to this "normal" behavior, as he has been doing the same thing for many years.)

Larry and Janet open their home and their hearts to all. As soon as you walk in their door, you feel like a part of the family. Janet enjoys telling about the occasions when Larry sees his former clients from the pharmacy. She is proud of how they always have a big hug and kind words for him.

Larry is also quite handy and enjoys working on the house. He has built a beautiful tiered flower garden, including a fountain, in their backyard for Janet to plant her many flowers. Larry enjoyed fly-fishing in the region's multitude of lakes and started to tie his own flies in the 1960s. He built his own cedar-strip canoe that they took out on the lakes, which he named R-KNU. Larry credits his handyman skills to his uncle Joe Hammerschmidt.

Joe was like an older brother to Larry and tutored him in plumbing, painting and carpentry work. Uncle Joe was a range finder in the Navy during World War II on a destroyer escort. It was his job to determine the distance for gunfire and depth charges to take out enemy submarines. Before Joe enlisted in the military, he owned a service station, where Larry enjoyed helping his uncle. After Joe got out of the service, he took jobs working on people's houses, painting and performing various improvements and maintenance. Larry would help him on these jobs, thus developing his own skills under Joe's guidance.

Larry posing in the canoe he made (R-KNU), supervised by his dog Sadie. Larry had Sadie for years. Even during her last days, after she became totally blind, she would still greet everyone at the door, always showing her affection. *(Courtesy Larry Kuntz)*

Because of his religious beliefs, Larry does not condone capital punishment. This may seem unusual coming from someone who had been stripped of a normal childhood with his parents. Violence and vengeance are not in his heart.

When the authors inquired of Larry how he managed to get through all the horrors of his early childhood, he replied that he gives the credit to a loving and protective family and the love of his wife and children as an adult. He also said he refused to ever let hatred ruin his life. Early on he made a decision to let go of the past and live for the future.

Larry returned to Columbus, Montana, in 1954, wanting to see the court records relating to the murders and the trial. The clerk at the courthouse abruptly turned him away, saying he didn't need to see them. He then stopped by the Atlas Bar in Columbus, where the bartender asked his name. When Larry told him who he was, the bartender gave him a beer and made mention that the night of the hanging of Frank Robideau was the busiest night they had ever had in Columbus.

Larry did not return to the Wheat Basin area until he and his family visited the Museum of the Beartooths in Columbus in 2010. They took the opportunity to travel to the site that used to be the town of Wheat Basin. This trip came about due to some investigating by Larry's grandson, Ambrose J. Cavegn III, known to his family as Josh. Josh was curious about his grandfather's past. He knew his great grandparents had died tragically at an early age, but no one ever talked about what had happened to them. Josh did some checking on the Internet and came across a man named Ken Mesch, who had purchased most of the property that once was home to the town of Wheat Basin. He uses the land and area for his passion of training falcons.

Interested in the history of the Wheat Basin area, Mesch decided to have a reunion of the former residents and anyone else that would like to attend. When Josh found this out, he contacted Ken and explained who he and his grandfather were. Ken was thrilled for the introduction to Josh, and to know that Larry Kuntz, "the little boy," was alive and well in Spokane. Many people in the Columbus area wondered what had become of him. Unbeknownst to the rest of the Kuntz family, Josh and Ken continued to correspond for some time. Josh finally asked Larry if Ken could contact him, and Larry agreed without hesitation.

About this same time, Larry attended his 60th class reunion in North Dakota. He was told by a relative that the Museum of the Beartooths in

Columbus had a display covering his parents' murders and the details of the Frank Robideau hanging. Penny Redli, the curator of the museum in Columbus, has put together a wonderful collection of the history of the area, which includes the especially interesting display of the Kuntz murders. A cousin thought Larry should see it and perhaps be able to receive some information that he had not previously been able to get. Ironically, about this time, another young family member in North Dakota had also been researching the topic and came across the name Ken Mesch. He gave the name to Larry's wife, Janet, and she began corresponding with Ken by e-mail, providing Ken with some current information about Larry. In 2010, Larry received a call from Ken Mesch inviting Larry, Janet, and their family to be his and his wife Lora's guests at their beautiful home in Columbus. They accepted his invitation, instantly gaining two new family friends in Ken and Lora.

When Larry and eight members of his family visited the museum, Penny Redli closed it to the public for the day. This allowed Larry and his family the privacy they needed to view the display and take in all the information stored there. Most of this was new and completely overwhelming to all of them.

Ken Mesch and his wife, Lora, It was Ken who helped Larry uncover information about that tragic night in Wheat Basin. Right, Larry holding the door latch used for his escape. *(Courtesy Janet Kuntz)*

After visiting the museum, Ken Mesch took the family out to what had once been the town of Wheat Basin, now reduced to old foundations, dirt, and weeds. Larry very vividly described where the general store had been, as well as the post office, the town Hall and the house where they lived, none of which existed anymore. While they were there, Larry went straight to the location where the Occident Grain Elevator once stood. The elevator had burned down in 1995, but Larry knew exactly where the door had been that he used to escape from the elevator and save his life.

Lost in thought as memories of so long ago flooded over him Larry started digging through the ashes and dirt. On his second day there, he found the latch he opened so many years ago to get out onto the loading platform. Larry took that latch home with him to Spokane. He feels it deserves a better place to rest than to be buried and lost amongst the dirt and ashes. After all, it helped save his life!

Ken Mesch felt it only appropriate that the Kuntz children should all have a part of what had been their father's past and that of the grandparents they never got to know. With that thought in mind, he gave them each a deed to a lot in what had once been the town of Wheat Basin, right where their father and his parents had lived 75 years ago.

In the summer of 2012, Larry received a phone call from a woman who explained that she had been researching her family's history and had found references to Larry. Her name was Cassandra Norman, and she informed Larry that Frank Robideau was her great-grandfather. She asked if they could meet, and Larry eagerly invited her to their home. During their visit and the many they have had since, Cassandra has learned what really happened those many years ago in Wheat Basin. She has come to be close friends with Larry and Janet and their family.

It was a relief for Larry to find out what had become of the Robideau family, as he had always felt bad for May and her children. He knew that whatever Frank Robideau had done was no fault of theirs. They, too, had been his victims.

It has been very therapeutic for Larry to be able to convey his feelings to a member of the Robideau family after all these years, with such a positive outcome. Things have come full-circle and, after 75 years, some healing and closure has finally begun to happen.

Museum of the Beartooths located in Columbus, Montana, where the Kuntz/Robideau exhibit is located. Penny Redli is the curator *(Hattenburg photo)*

From left: Becky Hattenburg, Larry Kuntz, Janet Kuntz, and Tim Hattenburg. This photo was taken on October 11, 2014, nearly 77 years after the tragic event. *(Bamonte photo)*

Larry and Janet Kuntz and their children, from left, Lori, Kristi, Lisa, and Mike. *(Courtesy Lisa Kuntz)*

Chapter Twelve

Epilogue

The story of the Kuntzes and Robideau made headlines in newspapers all over the area. A newspaper article in the May 19, 1938, *Columbus News* announced the "ROBIDEAU CASE IN NATIONAL MAGAZINE." The June issue of *Dynamic Detective Stories*, published by Country Press, Inc. of Louisville, Kentucky, contained a story written by Jack DeWitt, the pen name of Elbert Covington, a writer for the *Miles City Star*. The story was illustrated with photographs taken at the crime scene by Victor Murphy, son of Sheriff Murphy. It included a photo of Larry in the hospital. Newspapers from California, Texas, Washington, New York, Indiana, Utah, North Dakota, and Nevada carried the incredible story of the five-year-old Larry and the murder of his parents. Occasional articles contain references to the events of the murders to this day. Many of the writers failed to properly research the full account and, consequently, the articles often contain unchallenged references from Frank Robideau to the effect that Mike Kuntz was armed and threatened Frank.

May Robideau: In researching legal documents and in several newspaper accounts, we found that May Robideau's name was sometimes spelled "May" and other times "Mae." May is the correct spelling according to her relatives. Regardless of the spelling, May went through conditions that would break a weaker person. Throughout, she kept her head high and focused on her children.

The Stillwater County Commissioners minutes, from November 28, 1937, to January 15, 1938, show that $40 was approved to give to May Robideau and her three children for the purpose of moving May's home to Columbus.

Several years later, she met and married Lester Dennison, a mechanic from the Dodge dealership in Columbus. They moved with her children to The Dalles, Oregon. There were no children from her second marriage. Lester passed away in 1962. May passed away in 1991. They are both buried in the Dalles Oregon.

While May was still living in Columbus, the Plattsburgh National Bank and Trust Company of Plattsburgh, New York, sent a letter to May Robideau. However, it was addressed to Mrs. Joseph Liberty. She was trying to get the funds that had been left to Joseph Liberty by the estate of his father, John Liberty. The share that Joseph Liberty was to inherit was $83.79. May once again retained the services of Attorneys Blenkner and MacFarland, and letters went back and forth between the attorneys' office and officials in Plattsburgh, New York. Nothing could be found to determine if May ever received the money.

At the February 5, 1938, Stillwater County Commissioners' meeting, Edwin Meyers (May Robideau's brother-in-law) requested he be paid $30 for the care of the Robideau children. The commissioners disallowed the claim. Edwin and his wife took care of the children while May was in the hospital giving birth to her fourth child. Of course, at that time, Frank was in jail awaiting his execution.

Frank Robideau/Joseph Liberty: There are several things worthy of additional comment regarding this man. Of note is that neither the authorities nor the authors of this publication have much information regarding what Joseph did during the nearly eight-year gap between his fleeing New York and showing up in Wheat Basin for the final time. It is known he was in Wyoming, where he went by the name of Frank Johnson. Why he left that area so abruptly is another story. Did his pattern of destructive behavior lead him to also commit crimes there?

The other thing worthy of comment is that, despite the court being clearly aware that Frank Robideau was a fictitious name, the court and the press continued to refer to him as Frank Robideau. He was executed and buried under that name. His wife continued to use that name until she remarried.

Richard Robideau: Larry's playmate in Wheat Basin was born April 2, 1932, in Molt, Montana, to Frank and May (Dietzel) Robideau. He left Montana and moved to The Dalles with his mother. On April 29, 1955, he married Nancy Elizabeth Leabo in Stevenson, Washington. During the Korean War, Richard served his country in the U.S. Army. He was awarded the Bronze Star. He was extremely proud of his service to his country. Richard worked for the U.S. Army Corp. of Engineers in power-house operation for more than 30 years and retired in 1986. According to the *Hood River News*, he passed away at the family home in The Dalles Oregon on August 12, 2006. His wife and his four sons were at his side.

Sheriff John Franklin Murphy: If Sheriff Murphy was made to sound like a hero in this work, it is because he was. He was a remark-able man. Frank was born September 15, 1881, in Waco, Texas. His father passed away in Texas at an earlier date. Frank and his mother

VICTOR MURPHY FAMILY
Rear, left to right: Frank Murphy, Mrs. Frank Murphy, Mrs. Vic Murphy (holding Gordon), Vic Murphy.
Front: Michael and Honey Bea.

Sheriff Frank Murphy and his wife, Judith, with their son Victor and his family. Victor took all the photos at the crime scene, as well as the ones of Larry in the hospital. *(Courtesy Museum of the Beartooths)*

moved to Reed Point, Montana, when Frank was 13 years old. Murphy was married to Judith Mary Dillon of Roanoke, Virginia, on August 23, 1911, in Big Timber, Montana. The couple had three sons.

Before he became the sheriff of Stillwater County, Montana, he owned and operated a ranch just west of Reed Point. After selling the ranch, he took on the wholesale distribution of oil products. He became a deputy sheriff and the undersheriff in Columbus for Stillwater County prior to being elected sheriff. He served in that position for six years. This gave him 25 years duty as a lawman. People fondly remembered him as a fair and decent man who never acted like he was better than anyone else just because of his position in the community.

Being sheriff clearly was not an easy job. It did offer very good pay for the time. In 1937, Sheriff Frank Murphy received $166.66 per month salary. He was provided a residence, which was located next to the Stillwater County Courthouse. His granddaughter Judy Swarens can remember playing house in the jail cells when they were empty. The county also re-imbursed mileage and the care and feeding of prisoners. Murphy's wife, Judith, who prepared the meals for any of the prisoners housed there, was very well-liked by them because of her kind nature and excellent southern-style cooking.

According to the *Columbus News* of December 8, 1949, Sheriff Murphy served as Stillwater County Sheriff from 1936 until 1943. He was forced to retire due to a paralytic stroke in 1943. Sadly, he remained in poor health until his death on December 4, 1949.

Murphy was a very religious man who did not believe in capital punishment, although he steadfastly carried out his duties as sheriff concerning Robideau's sentence. His family and friends expressed their certainty that the terrible murders and the hanging had an adverse effect on his health. They felt that he was never quite the same afterwards. He died at age 68 and was buried in the Mountain View Cemetery in Columbus, Montana. His widow, his three sons and their wives, and eight grandchildren survived him.

Undersheriff Jack S. Benjamin: Jack came to Montana from Nebraska. Prior to his move, he served with the U.S. Army in the Spanish-American War, and in the Philippine Island campaign. Upon his arrival in Stillwater County, he homesteaded a ranch west of Rapelje. He was active in organizing a bank in Rapelje. Later, he moved his wife, Meda, and two daughters, Aleva and Dorothy, to Columbus. Benjamin served as Stillwater County undersheriff and later as sheriff for several years. He then moved to Helena, where he held an administrative position with the Montana State Liquor Control Board until poor health forced his retirement. He passed away on December 31, 1946.

Herschel Slavens: Herschel was the owner of Slavens Lumber and Mercantile in Molt, Montana, which carried groceries, lumber, hardware, machinery, gasoline, and housed the post office. Herschel Slavens was appointed postmaster of Molt in 1932, a position he held for 35 years, retiring in 1967.

Slavens Store and Lumber Yard located in Molt, Montana, where Frank Robideau cashed his check the day after he killed Mike and Frieda Kuntz. *(Courtesy Museum of the Beartooths)*

On November 17, 1945, Mr. Slavens received a letter from the National War Finance Committee commending him for selling a total of $101,131.75 in Series E War Savings Bonds. The Occident Elevator and blacksmith shop closed in the 1930s leaving Molt Farmers Elevator Co. and Slavens Store the only remaining businesses, which they remain today. The Slavens Store was sold to Dwight Kepferle in 1968.

Florence Bowie: Florence, the only woman to witness the hanging, when she disguised herself as a man, was known to many of her childhood friends as Flora. She was an only child. Her mother always took great pride in curling her long hair into ringlets, and always had her wear long, pretty dresses. When her mother died, she traded in her dresses for men's overalls and shirts. Flora cut off all her curls and, from then on, wore her hair in a man's short-style cut. She was well known for her horsemanship and took over the family property on the Yellowstone River when her father passed away.

Due to unfortunate circumstances, she eventually lost the property and moved to a small place on Kaiser Creek, where she raised sheep and tried to scratch out a living. Even as she struggled to get by, some of her childhood friends dug a well for her and gave her clothing. This included a pair of shoes when townspeople noticed that she had no soles in her old worn shoes. Florence died in 1993.

Bob Harsha: The 16-year-old who witnessed the hanging from outside of the building is currently 94 years old. He still owns and operates his barbershop in downtown Columbus today. When not cutting hair, Bob enjoys golfing with his many friends. He is the only known living eyewitness to the hanging!

The Kuntzes' Car: After the hanging, Mike's brother Val Kuntz drove Mike's car back to Richardton, North Dakota. It was a cold drive for Val that January, especially with the bullet holes in the windows. On his way home, Val stopped at a motel in Madora, North Dakota, to spend the night. When the owner of the motel saw the condition of the car, he met Val with a gun. Val explained to the man how the 1930 Chevrolet came to be in its present condition, and all was well after that. That spring Val's wife cleaned up the car and it was sold, with the money going to Larry.

Val's grandson, Clayton Kuntz, recently tried to track down the car with the hopes of recovering it and donating it to the Museum of the Beartooths in Columbus, Montana. Clayton was able to trace the car to Mott, North Dakota, where it had been stored in a building. Unfortunately, that building had burned down and the car was destroyed in the fire.

The Atlas Bar: The bar, located in Columbus, Montana, was the gathering place for all the out-of-towners who came for the hanging. It still stands today and is on the historical register. In 1959 the bar got a new owner (the son of the original owner) and was named the New Atlas Bar. It is open for business in downtown Columbus. To this day, the largest crowd they have ever had was on the night of the hanging.

The Atlas Bar, now the New Atlas Bar, as it appears today, is located in downtown Columbus, Montana. It has always been a great gathering place for locals and visitors alike. *(Hattenburg photo)*

The Galloping Gallows: The gallows were later moved to Deer Lodge, Montana, where they have now been officially retired. They are housed inside the Powell County Museum and Arts Foundation building, where they serve as a grim example of early western justice.

They are one of the few original hanging gallows remaining in the United States. The gallows were first used in Forsyth, September 3, 1920, to execute Alfred Lane for the murder of a local rancher. The gallows served as the official hanging scaffold for eastern Montana. They were designed to be easily taken apart, "galloped to the new site," then rebuilt in a new location. The main parts of the scaffold are marked with matching numbers to ease reconstruction. Thus arose the nickname of "Galloping Gallows." During 20 years of use, a total of seven men were executed using the gallows. (Frank Robideau was number six.) The last use was in 1939. In 1978, the gallows was sent to be used in Great Falls, Montana. Because of delays and postponements in that scheduled execution, they were never used for any hangings after 1939.

The Metal Building: The building where the execution took place still stands today. It is on the corner of Diamond Street and First Avenue North and is part of a thriving business owned by Alvin Stadel and Harry Harsha. They have updated the outside of the building, replacing the old hole-studded tin siding with new metal siding. They now operate their company, Stadel and Harsha Construction, out of the building. They lovingly refer to it as the "Hang Out."

George Liberty: After his release from prison, George returned to Plattsburgh and became a cook in a local restaurant. He met and married Annie in 1928. She was three years his senior. According to the 1930 U.S. Federal Census, they rented their home for $15 per month, and Annie worked as a cook in a hotel. They did not have any children. George died in 1960 at the age of 68 in Plattsburgh, and is buried at St. Peters Cemetery. There is no evidence or any indication that he had any trouble with the law after his release from prison.

Newell Varno: Newell was a Civil War veteran and served with Company H, 16th Regiment, New York. He was discharged June 25, 1865. Even though the Varnos were a very poor family, they were remarkable in that their father, along with his four sons, served their country during the Civil War. The family saw extensive front-line action. Even more remarkable is the fact that they all survived and were honorably discharged from service.

The private hospital room where Newell was taken after the shooting was paid for by a prominent local citizen of Plattsburgh, New York, who himself had been a member of the Grand Army of the Republic (Union Army). Newell and his brother David Varno are buried at the St. Peters Cemetery. They are in unmarked graves due to the lack of family finances at the time of their passing.

Auburn Prison: Auburn Correctional Facility is a state prison on State Street in Auburn, New York. It is located on land that once was the home of a Cayuga Indian village and is classified as a maximum-security facility. Constructed in 1816, it became the second state prison built in New York. Newgate Prison in New York City was the first and was operated from 1797-1828. Auburn is currently the oldest prison in operation today.

This is where the "Auburn System" for the treatment of inmates was developed. This system was an infamous method used in the 1820s in which the inmates were worked in groups during the day at various hard-labor tasks and were then kept in solitary confinement at night. The prisoners were segregated according to the type of crime they committed. The traditional prison uniform consisting of horizontal black and white stripes originated here. The inmates had their hair closely cropped, and they were forced to walk in lockstep with their heads bowed. They were forbidden from making eye contact with the guards or one another.

Strictly enforced silence was kept at all times. Silence was the most significant factor in the many rules the prisoners had to follow. The premise was that the lack of speaking would take away a person's "sense of self," making them more compliant and obedient to the warden's wishes.

The second characteristic of the system was that there be strictly regimented community activities during the day. The inmates would have various tasks to perform such as making nails, clothing, shoes and boots, carpets, buttons, carpenter tools, and even steam engines and boilers.

During the 1840s, the prison even got into the silk-making business by bringing in silkworms and trees. The Auburn facility was the first prison to profit from the labor of the prisoners. The prison even had sightseers who paid a fee to tour the grounds and the facilities. As can be imagined, the zoo-like tour visits by total strangers made inmate life even more unbearable, as they were taunted by the constant flow of free people coming and going at will.

Punishment was severe, and flogging was common for even minor infractions. When Elam Lynds became warden in 1821, he frequently used the power of the whip for discipline. During his tenure as warden, many inmates died from the abuse of flogging by the whip.

The first person in the world to be executed by the electric chair was at Auburn prison on August 6, 1890. William Kemmler was convicted of first-degree murder, and was sentenced to die for the brutal murder of his common-law wife, Matilda Ziegler. Records show, on March 29, 1889, Kemmler went on one of his drunken "binges." When confronted by Matilda, he grabbed a hatchet off a nearby counter and killed her. He never denied the crime and went to the chair wishing the executioner good luck in his role. Leon Czolgosz, the assassin of President William McKinley, also went to the same electric chair for his devious act and was executed on October 29, 1901.

Many reforms have taken place over the years, and the "Auburn System" is now a distant memory. Prisons nationwide grapple with the discipline and rehabilitation of their inmates on a daily basis. Security guards, as well as civilian staff, have the daunting task of encountering extremely challenging situations 24 hours and day and seven days a week and deserve the gratitude of all of us whom they protect through their service.

In a dramatic proof of the maxim, "It is a small world," there is an intersection of this story and the lives of the people. The stepfather of Ian Graham, Warrington Russell "Bill" Willis, was a young boy living in Auburn at the time of the Liberty escape. His father was Cayuga County prosecutor. One day in 1922, a man came into the back yard while Bill was playing there. He eyed the freshly hung laundry and asked the young boy if he could have a shirt, as he had none. Bill agreed, and the man went on his way with a new shirt. Bill's parents were quite put out, as the shirt the man took was his father's best. It turned out that the man was a prison escapee.

Clinton Correctional Facility: The largest maximum-security prison in New York is located in the village of Dannemora, about 15 miles west of the town of Plattsburgh on New York State Route 374. The prison, the third oldest facility of its kind in New York, is often incorrectly referred to as Dannemora because of its proximity to the town. The actual name is derived from its location in Clinton County, New York. The southern perimeter of the prison wall borders Route 374 and, as the town is approached, the daunting wall which is around 40 feet high, stands out above everything in the surrounding area. The enormity of the entire

Welcoming sign to the village of Dannemora, New York with a depiction of the prison wall in the center. *(Hattenburg photo)*

Present-day town of Dannemora, directly across from the imposing wall that surrounds Clinton Correctional Facility. *(Hattenburg photo)*

structure stands as a reminder of the magnitude and importance the facility plays in that area.

Built in 1844, the Clinton facility originally served as a site where prisoners were used to work in the local mines in both Dannemora and nearby Lyons Mountain. Because of its isolated location and cold climate, it is sometimes referred to as "Little Siberia." Pete Light, a retired correctional officer and founder of a museum located in that facility, pointed out the prison served not only as a place of employment but as part of a longtime family tradition. Most everyone who lived in the village, at one time or the other, worked there.

The structure began as a small outpost prison with a few small buildings surrounded by a wooden stockade fence. As the number of inmates increased, the fence was replaced with stone. According to Light, the old stone cut for the original wall came from Lyons Mountain. Years later, as the prison continued to expand, the stone wall was replaced with the high concrete walls and the enclosed guard towers that ominously overlook the prison yard today.

Clinton Correctional Facility was originally built to house around 500 inmates. The facility has grown to hold more than 2,700, and employs about 980 officers. Employees were originally required to live in the vil-

Photo of Moses Goodrich (1880). Mr. Goodrich and his ox cart were a familiar sight around Dannemora, as he sold water to both the prison and village inhabitants. In the background is the wooden fence that originally surrounded the prison grounds between 1884 and 1887. This fence was replaced by a stone wall at a cost of $20,000. *(Hattenburg photo of a photo)*

lage, so they could be close in the event of any major problems occurring inside the walls. As transportation improved, more people from outside of Dannemora began to work at the facility.

In 1899, a mental health facility, the Dannemora State Hospital, was built on the grounds to house prisoners that became insane while serving their time there. If inmates were still deemed insane following the completion of their sentence, they were kept in custody at the hospital.

Ironically, during the late 1890s and early 1900s, Dannemora became a choice of many criminals throughout New York State's population due to a nationwide outbreak of tuberculosis. Doctors in other prisons would recommend that inmates be sent there because the fresh air of the Adirondacks was known to help them breathe much easier. By 1941 the demand for a larger hospital led to the construction of the current Dannemora State Hospital. It was built to accommodate 200 inmates and served as a general doctor's office, a psychiatric facility, and tuber-

Aerial view of Dannemora and the Clinton Correctional facility, where George and Joseph Liberty were taken after their murder conviction in New York. Circa 1930. *(Photos Courtesy Pete Light)*

Clinton Correctional facility on New York Route 374, circa 1940.

culosis hospital. Following the development of new medications during the 1940s, the number of tuberculosis patients slowly began to decline. Today the hospital continues its daily operations as a dental facility and general hospital.

Harsh treatment of prisoners was not unusual in the 1800s and Clinton followed the practices of the "Auburn System" as well. There were originally no bathing facilities, and the prisoners wore the striped uniforms as in Auburn. Some officers were fond of using a leather paddle and would tie unruly inmates to the floor and beat them for their violations of behavior code.

Ball and chain, circa 1910, similar to ones used at Clinton Prison to keep prisoners in control and unable to escape. *(Hattenburg photo)*

By 1900, many forms of this type of punishment were abandoned, with the notable exception of the electric chair. Twenty-six men were executed in the chair before it was discontinued at the prison in 1913. The New York State Legislature decreed that any further executions would be carried out at Sing Sing Prison in New York City. The death penalty was abolished in the state of New York in 1965.

Over the years, the prison has been plagued by a series of fires and life-threatening rebellions. The most infamous riot took place on July 22, 1929, when over 1,300 inmates made a desperate attempt to escape by charging the prison walls. After setting fire to their lumber supply and other buildings, the desperate convicts took their aggression out on the guards. Many of the guards were captured, stoned, and beaten. Three of them met their death at the hands of the angry mob.

Prison officials called upon the help of state troopers, as well as the 20th Infantry. The riot continued throughout the afternoon. Upon the arrival of state troopers armed with a wide array of weaponry, including grenades and various kinds of guns and ammunition, most of the inmates surrendered. A hard-core group of as many as 100 inmates barricaded themselves in the tailor shop. When the warden presented them with an ultimatum to surrender or die, they surrendered.

Electric chair used at Clinton prison, circa 1910. This was the punishment avoided by the Liberty brothers with their second-degree instead of a first-degree murder sentencing. *(Courtesy Pete Light)*

Over the years the numbers of violent and deadly incidents have cost the lives of many guards who gave their service to the prison in order to maintain the peace behind the sometimes-deadly walls.

Mormon Crickets: In 1937, there was a horrible infestation over much of the West which newspapers referred to as "Mormon Crickets." These crickets and grasshoppers were consuming what little wheat there was. According to Dr. Harlo B. Mills, state entomologist at Montana State College in Bozeman, the state of Montana had the worst infestation of "Mormon crickets." Forty-five percent of all the acreage in the seven western states that were overrun by them was in Montana.

Cricket-control work in Wheat Basin and Stillwater County began the 1st of May and continued through the middle of August. During this period, 50,000 pounds of sodium arsenate dust and 40,000 pounds of wet bait (to keep the eggs from hatching) were spread on 10,000 acres of cropland. The crickets were so dense in some areas of the county that farmers in the Flaherty Flat area resorted to the use of fire guns and flame-throwers in an attempt to stave off further encroachment of the pests. For several weeks it was also necessary to apply oil in the ditches to prevent crickets from crossing into the irrigated lands of the lower Stillwater and Flaherty Flat. When the crickets would cover the roads, they created a very slick surface that made driving quite hazardous.

The farmers and the county shared equally the cost of this effort to rid the area of crickets and grasshoppers. The County Extension agent's report also indicated that without federal funds for labor costs it would have been extremely difficult to carry out the cricket-control campaigns. In Stillwater County, a total of $14,331.14 (approximately $232,000 in today's money) in federal funds was used to hire 153 men. Farmers living in the cricket-infested areas were given priority in filling out the work crews. The pay from these jobs helped the farmers cover their share of the costs for the pest-control program.

Without control of the cricket areas, the crops would have been totally destroyed, and it would not have been cost effective to even try to harvest what was left in the fields. As it was, some farmers were only able to harvest up to 20 bushels per acre. A study done by Dr. Mills showed that the "Hopper Campaign of 1937" saved the state of Montana $2 million worth of crops (equal to over $32 million today) from grasshoppers and $5 million worth of crops (equal to $81 million today) from the Mormon crickets.

Wheat Basin: In 1915, homesteaders Dave and Hugh Williams, originally from Nora, Illinois, christened the town of Nora, Montana. It was located in the eastern part of the state, midway between the towns of Molt and Rapelje. The nearest towns of any size were those of Columbus and the much larger city of Billings. When the Northern Pacific rail spur was completed in the summer of 1917, the Riopel family had opened a mercantile store in Nora. As the town continued to grow, the postal service in Washington, D.C., placed a post office in the Riopel Mercantile Store. Francis Riopel became the first postmistress in town. This occurred when the U.S. Postal Service in Washington, D.C., informed her there was already a town with the name of Nora. Francis Riopel replied to the Postal Service, requesting that the name be changed from Nora to Wheat Basin.

In 1919, J. J. Stolte recorded the town plat of Wheat Basin, which was reported to have a population of over 100 residents and businesses that included the Farmers State Bank, Simpkins Lumber Company, Clark Lumber Company, two general stores, a pool hall, two grain elevators, and a new school. There were two churches under construction, along with the Lutgen Brothers Garage/Blacksmith Shop. There was also a community building, known as Stillwater Hall, which had originally been built by area residents as a local project before Nora was founded. It was originally located on the Reuben Castle homestead and was moved to the town of Wheat Basin in 1920.

In the mid 1920s, oil was discovered in the Hepp Field eight miles to the south. Wheat Basin soon became an important shipping destination for the drilling companies. Casings, drill bits, steam boilers, and timbers for the construction of oil derricks were shipped to the town, and then hauled to the oil fields by teams and wagons. The rail-head was also a boon to the many local farmers in the area for shipping their grain, the population of Molt, Rapelje, and Wheat Basin swelled to around 1,000.

The oil-building boom soon passed, and by the late 1920s, the oil fields were not shipping any supplies through Wheat Basin. Coupled with the continued failure of sizable crop yields, by the spring of 1937 the town of Wheat Basin had become a quiet, peaceful, and somewhat-isolated community. The town site was made up of approximately 60 residents, consisting mostly of the store owners and their families. The surrounding rural area was made up of wheat farmers, living on farms ranging in size from 200 to 1,000 acres of land.

The location where Wheat Basin once stood. All that can be seen of the former town are ruts where roads once were and a few old foundations of buildings. *(Hattenburg photo)*

A 1959 photo of the Occident Grain Elevator in Wheat Basin. This picture came from Maxine Crouch, of Columbus, who lived in Wheat Basin as a child. *(Courtesy the* Columbus News*)*

All that remains of the Occident Elevator are the metal supports for the scales and cement foundations after a fire burned it to the ground in 1995. *(Hattenburg photo)*

Today, a person would have to look hard to realize that a town ever stood in the location of Wheat Basin. Looking closely, in the midst of the sagebrush, evidence of streets and a few foundations of the old buildings can be seen. A few of the old buildings, although no longer located in Wheat Basin, are still in use. The dance hall, whose last recorded dance was held in 1952, was gifted to Molt Farmers Elevator and was moved to the town of Molt. It is currently being used as a community center. The school was hauled to the town of Fishtail, where it is being used as a shop. The blacksmith shop was moved to a property closer to Rapelje. The Catholic church ended up as part of a house in the Blue Creek area of Billings. The mercantile store was dismantled and the lumber sent by train to California for use in building two houses. The safe from the town's bank is now located in Columbus at the New Atlas Bar. The Occident Grain Elevator burned to the ground in 1995. All that remains is a foundation and the scales that held the Kuntzes car following their murder.

Plattsburgh, New York: In 2010, the population was 11,870 within the city limits. However, in the greater Plattsburgh area, which includes all communities residing in the immediate Clinton County area, it was 82,128.

Following Samuel de Champlain's expedition into the Lake Champlain Valley in 1609, this region was under French rule. The proximity to Quebec and Montreal reinforced the French influence.

There was an extensive fur-trading network throughout the area, with the city of Montreal as the hub. French missionaries began to settle alongside the indigenous populations where native villages were found. Plattsburgh and the lands comprising much of present-day Clinton County were originally part of the French settlement of New France.

The French lost control of the area after their defeat at the hands of the British at the conclusion of the French and Indian War in 1763. The British lost control of the area at the end of the American Revolution in 1783, and conceded the territory to the newly established United States of America in the Treaty of Paris.

Zephaniah Platt founded the city after George Clinton granted him the land to buffer emerging American interests in the Saint Lawrence River Valley and the Lake Champlain Valley. The local residents have exercised their unique French culture in one obvious way. There is no "Main Street," as the major streets and thoroughfares are named after the

Downtown Plattsburgh just blocks from the Clinton County Courthouse. Buildings were constructed in the 1880s-90s. *(Hattenburg photo)*

St. Peter's Church in present day Plattsburgh. The Varnos and the Libertys were members of this parish. George Liberty, David and Newell Varno are all buried at the St. Peter's Cemetery. *(Hattenburg photo)*

daughters of prominent businessmen and local politicians. In a similar fashion, local streets are named after such famous Frenchmen as Champlain and General Louis-Joseph de Montcalm.

Because of its location near a major waterway, and the proximity to the Canadian border, Plattsburgh was the site of some major historic events. Two prominent ones were the Battle of Valcour Island during the Revolutionary War and the Battle of Plattsburgh during the War of 1812. During the Cold War, Plattsburgh Air Force Base (PAFB) was activated and housed missile silos for our ICBM (Intercontinental Ballistic Missile Defense System). It was the home of the 556 Strategic Missile Squadron.

The 380th Bombardment Aerospace and Refueling Wings were also stationed here. This included B-52 bombers, air-refueling tankers, and FB-111s. Despite the numerous awards for excellent performance, PABF was closed down on September 29, 1995, in a round of national base closures.

Today the city relies on new industries that have sprung up in the area. Bombardier, Nova Bus, and the Georgia-Pacific paper plant are major employers.

During the month of May, a person could stroll down to the city park on the Saranac River and watch fly fisherman in their waders casting for migrating salmon as they make their journey upriver from Lake Champlain to spawn. Plattsburgh is a town that is very easy to find your way around, and it is easy to take in the many historical sites, as well as the local businesses and various restaurants.

The Saranac River, downtown Plattsburgh, flows into Lake Champlain seen in the background. *(Hattenburg photo)*

Bibliography and Sources

Annin, Jim They Gazed on the Beartooths and Eighty Years of Memories on the Banks of the Yellowstone, pages 198-201

Billings Public Library

Clinton County Historian's Office, Plattsburgh, New York

Coroners Inquest Records, courtesy Museum of the Beartooths, Columbus, MT.

Death Certificates, courtesy Stillwater County Courthouse records department

Dr. Anastasia Pratt, Clinton County Historian, Plattsburgh, New York

Fargo Forum, Fargo, North Dakota

Glen Whitely, retired Spokane County Sheriff's Office, crime scene photographer,   Identification of cars in photos

Hooker, Patty Moccasins, Mining and Montana's 34th County, pages 132,133

Letters of correspondence by Attorneys Blenkner and MacFarlane on behalf of Frank   Robideau, courtesy Museum of the Beartooths

Letters witten by Michael Kuntz to his brother Val Kuntz in 1937, and his sister in Oct.   1937, courtesy of Larry and Richard Kuntz

McCarthy, Don Afternoons in Montana, 1971, pages 23-34

McGraw Hill Publishing, From Sea to Shining Sea, 1982

Mountain West Voices with Clay Scott

NNYACGS – Genealogy and Family History Library, Plattsburgh, New York

Northern New York Library Network

Swenson, Ella The Courage of a Pioneer Woman, pages 50-51

The Dickinson Press, Dickinson, ND Dec. 9, 1937, Dec. 16, 1937, Jan. 20,1938, Dec. 2, 1937, Dec. 30, 1937, Nov. 27, 1937, Jan. 13,1938

The Essex County Republican, New York Dec. 23, 1910 and various issues

The Museum of the Beartooths, Columbus, MT., Penny Redli, curator

The Plattsburgh Republican, Plattsburgh, NY, January 17,1938

The Plattsburgh Sentinel, Plattsburgh, NY various issues from 1910 and 1924

The Spokesman Review, Spokane, Washington Nov.28, 1937, Nov.30, 1937, Dec. 1, 1937, Dec. 2, 1937, Dec. 3, 1937, Dec, 16, 1937, Jan. 16, 1938

Treasurers Office, County of Clinton, Plattsburgh, New York Sept. 1, 1938

Peterson, Gwen Big Sky Stories, page 16

Internet Websites:

Ancestry,com, TimeAndDate.com, Wikipedia, Findagrave.com

The following people provided interviews:

Norma Cook
Bob Harsha
Margaret Holgren
Rod Hubner
Clayton Kuntz
Larry Kuntz
Janet Kuntz
Richard Kuntz
Pete Light
Bob Murphy
Barbara Orr
Anastasia Pratt, PhD
John Robideau
Judy Swarens

Index